Current Perspectives in Psychology

Delinquency, Development, and Social Policy

David Brandt

YALE UNIVERSITY PRESS   NEW HAVEN AND LONDON

Set in Adobe Garamond type by The Composing Room of Michigan, Inc.
Printed in the United States of America.

Library of Congress Cataloging-in-Publication Data
Brandt, David.
Delinquency, development, and social policy / David Brandt.
p.   cm. — (Current perspectives in psychology)
Includes bibliographical references and index.
ISBN 0-300-10894-X (cloth : alk. paper)
1. Juvenile delinquents—Mental health.   2. Juvenile delinquents—
Rehabilitation—United States.   3. Juvenile delinquency—United States—
Prevention.   4. Juvenile delinquency—Social aspects—United States.
I. Title. II. Series.
RJ506.J88B74 2006
364.36—dc22
2005010510

A catalogue record for this book is available from the British Library.
The paper in this book meets the guidelines for permanence and durability
of the Committee on Production Guidelines for Book Longevity of the
Council on Library Resources.

10 9 8 7 6 5 4 3 2 1

To my family

"Gee, Officer Krupke"

ACTION *(to Diesel)*
Dear kindly judge, your honor,
My parents treat me rough.
With all their marijuana,
They won't give me a puff.
They didn't wanna have me,
But somehow I was had.
Leapin' lizards! That's why I'm so bad!
DIESEL *(imitating judge)* Right!
Officer Krupke, you're really a square;
This boy don't need a judge, he needs an analyst's care!
It's just his neurosis that oughta be curbed.
He's psychologic'ly disturbed!
ACTION
I'm disturbed!
JETS
We're disturbed, we're disturbed,
We're the most disturbed,
Like we're psychologic'ly disturbed.
DIESEL *(imitating judge)* In the opinion of this court, this child is
    depraved on account he ain't had a normal home.
ACTION Hey I'm depraved on account I'm deprived!
DIESEL So take him to a headshrinker.
ACTION *(Sings)*
My father is a bastard,
My ma's an S.O.B.
My grandpa's always plastered,
My grandma pushes tea.
My sister wears a mustache,
My brother wears a dress.
Goodness gracious, that's why I'm a mess!
A-RAB *(imitating psychiatrist)* Yes!
Officer Krupke, you're really a slob.
This boy don't need a doctor, just a good steady job.
Society's played him a terrible trick,
And sociologic'ly he's sick!
ACTION
I am sick!
ALL
We are sick, we are sick,
We are sick, sick, sick,

Like we're sociologically sick!

A-RAB *(imitating psychiatrist)* In my opinion, this child don't need to
    have his head shrunk at all. Juvenile delinquency is purely a social
    disease!

ACTION Hey, I got a social disease!

A-RAB *(psychiatrist)* So take him to a social worker!

ACTION *(to Baby John)*
Dear kindly social worker,
They say go earn a buck.
Like be a soda jerker,
Which means like be a schmuck.
It's not I'm antisocial,
I'm only antiwork.
Gloryosky, that's why I'm a jerk!

BABY JOHN *(imitating female social worker, in falsetto)*
Eek!
Officer Krupke, you've done it again.
This boy don't need a job, he needs a year in the pen.
It ain't just a question of misunderstood;
Deep down inside him, he's no good!

ACTION
I'm no good!

ALL
We're no good, we're no good,
We're no earthly good,
Like the best of us is no damn good!

DIESEL *(judge)*
The trouble is he's crazy.

A-RAB *(psychiatrist)*
The trouble is he drinks.

BABY JOHN *(female social worker)*
The trouble is he's lazy.

DIESEL *(judge)*
The trouble is he stinks.

A-RAB *(psychiatrist)*
The trouble is he's growing.

BABY JOHN *(social worker)*
The trouble is he's grown.

ALL
Krupke, we got trouble of our own!
Gee, Officer Krupke,
We're down on our knees,
'Cause no one wants a fellow with a social disease.
Gee, Officer Krupke,
What are we to do?
Gee, Officer Krupke.
Krup you!

Contents

Series Foreword

Current Perspectives in Psychology presents the latest discoveries and developments across the spectrum of the psychological and behavioral sciences. The series explores such important topics as learning, intelligence, trauma, stress, brain development and behavior, anxiety, interpersonal relationships, education, child rearing, divorce and marital discord, and child, adolescent, and adult development. Each book focuses on critical advances in research, theory, methods, and applications and is designed to be accessible and informative to nonspecialists and specialists alike.

In this book, Dr. David Brandt presents key issues concerning delinquency. The topics include a statement of what delinquency is, what is known about the causes, risk, and protective factors, treatment and prevention programs, the adjudication process, and more. The book moves logically through these topics by considering the emergence and course of delinquency over development and how delinquency is treated in society. Treatment not only includes interventions designed to overcome delinquency but also the judicial and legal responses to individuals identified as delinquent. Strengths and limitations of treatment and prevention programs and judicial practices are highlighted and evaluated. The findings at once convey progress in developing effective practices but also needed directions for research.

Distinguishing features of this book are many. First, this is a concise statement that conveys what we know and what can be done about the problem. There is a sense of completion in reading this book as it moves systematically from clarifying what the problems of delinquency are and what is, can, and ought to be done about it. Within a concise space, the author has provided a book broad in scope. Second, the type of coverage is noteworthy. Although research is covered, this is not a research book of all the findings of delinquency. The author presents considerable research and certainly the main findings of what is known. Yet the findings are made more concrete by including case vignettes, social issues that emerge in adjudicating youths, and issues of everyday life for the delinquent. Finally, the book reflects the benefit of many interactions the author has had working in the system. Contacts with family court judges, advocates, administrators, social scientists, and others involved in delinquency give a perspective that is critical for understanding the nature of the problem. This, in addition to his own extensive experience, provides a work that is astute, informed, and without peer. We are extremely fortunate to have this book in light of the coverage, engaging style, and authoritativeness.

Alan E. Kazdin
Series Editor

Preface

As I sat in the back row of the family court in Rochester, New York, a fourteen-year-old girl diagnosed with bipolar disorder, who was being held in detention on a PINS (person in need of supervision) petition brought by her mother, was telling the judge that she wanted to go home. The judge told her that because of her behavior problems at the residence where she was staying, that was not possible, but that it would be possible for her mother to take her out to dinner a few nights out of the week. The judge, addressing the girl's mother, asked, "Would that be okay, Mom?" The mother replied, less than enthusiastically, "If it doesn't cost too much." The girl, who was standing before the judge, turned to her mother and said rather plaintively, "We could eat at home." Mom demurred, saying that it would create problems with her (the mother's) boyfriend. The girl was led away in handcuffs.

The parents of the next adolescent appearing before the court did not show up for the hearing. The mother of the youngster who appeared after that was in jail. I asked the judge's law clerk, who was sitting next to me, why these kids were all in handcuffs. He said they would run away otherwise and wouldn't appear for their hearing. He also told me that the whole system is overwhelmed, and that he himself couldn't sit through a whole session because it was too painful. I noted to myself that nobody seemed to want these kids and that it wasn't clear, despite the official proceedings, that anyone was sure what to do with them. This is just the tip of the iceberg. This scenario is repeated, with slight variation, in thousands of juvenile courts across the country. The youngsters' stories are incredibly painful to listen to. Their realities are hidden behind statistics and "data" and countless numbers of research studies which do not adequately communicate their plight.

In addition to my work as a clinical psychologist, in which I frequently work with adolescents, I am a psychology professor at John Jay College of Criminal Justice, which is part of the City University of New York. Fifteen years ago I developed a course on the psychology and treatment of juvenile delinquents with my colleague Jack Zlotnick, for our Master's-level program in forensic psychology. Since at that time just about all courses on delinquency were being taught by sociologists in departments of criminal justice, our course was somewhat unusual. Teaching a graduate course requires that I keep up with the recent research in the field. In the following pages, I present studies which illustrate the points I want to make by providing examples of how social scientists and others are addressing the problem of antisocial behavior in young people. Written for a general audience, this book is not meant to provide a detailed or comprehensive overview of the field of delinquency. Those readers interested in a more in-depth look at the issues I raise can consult the list of additional readings at the end of the book. The case histories that I present are based on the lives of real adolescents, although I have changed the names and places. Many of the case histories were provided to me by my colleagues at the psychology department, some are from my own practice, and others are from newspaper accounts. However, it is important to bear in mind that case histories illustrate points; they don't prove them.

In the first chapter I describe the problems associated with defining and measuring juvenile delinquency. While one might conclude that this would be straightforward, it is actually complex, because the definitions are relative and information regarding the frequency of delinquent behavior is not completely valid. In the second and third chapters I provide an overview of what is understood about how children and adolescents become delinquent. There is, and has been for a long time, a substantial amount of agreement about the factors that are associated with the development of delinquent behavior. In chapter 4 I discuss judicial/legal responses to juvenile delinquency and give an overview of some of the psychological interventions that have been developed to modify this behavior in adolescents. The judicial/legal response, at the very least, seems very much in need of reform. And while psychological interventions have improved over recent years, there are still many adolescents who do not benefit from them. In chapter 5 I provide a description of risk factors and precursors of adolescent delinquency followed by an overview of some programs designed to prevent delinquency. Prevention of delinquency is likely to be our best hope, a point made in a recent report by the Surgeon General of the United States.

In researching this book, I've had the opportunity to talk with family court judges, program administrators, politicians, advocates, and attorneys for young people. I have come to realize that social scientists alone cannot solve the problem and should not remain isolated from the political processes that are ultimately responsible for policy reform. My hope is that this book will get people to think about juvenile delinquents not just as statistics, or as bad kids behaving badly, but also as the victims of neglect by those responsible for their care, which includes all of us.

Acknowledgments

A number of people provided help, input, and support while I was writing this book. I would like to thank Marjorie Cohen for her careful reading of the manuscript. Her editorial suggestions were invaluable. Mishi Faruquee and Margret Loftus of the Juvenile Justice Project of the New York Corrections Association were kind enough to allow me to attend their Advocacy Day in Albany, New York, and spent time talking to me about the problems in juvenile justice. The gracious hospitality of Assemblyman Joseph Errigo, who introduced me to other members of the New York State Assembly, was beyond what I could have reasonably anticipated. A number of individuals were kind enough to take time out of their busy schedules to talk to me. Among them were State Senator Eric Schniderman; Assemblyman Scott Stringer; Ron Richter, Deputy Director of the Juvenile Division of the Legal Aid Society; Paul Donnely, a former juvenile justice official; and Dirk Hightower of the Children's Institute in Rochester, New York. I would also like to thank Judge Alex Renzi for allowing me to sit in on his family court session. Professors Stuart Kirschner, Louis Schlessinger, and Mathew Johnson, all excellent forensic psychologists, were kind enough to provide me with useful case materials. And finally the editor of this series, Alan Kazdin, provided long-distance support and encouragement. I thank them all. I would also like to thank the editorial staff at Yale University Press for their help in the final preparation of the manuscript.

Delinquency, Development, and Social Policy

1

Definitions and Measures

A definition is the enclosing a wilderness of idea within a wall of words.
Samuel Butler

When he was just fifteen years old, barely shaving, Bryan was charged by the police in a large urban city with the following crimes: murder in the second degree, robbery in the first degree, burglary in the first degree, and criminal possession of a weapon in the first and second degree. He lived with his mother, who suffered from AIDS and bone cancer, an older brother, and a cousin. Bryan had had academic problems dating from the beginning of his school career. He was frequently truant and was diagnosed as having attention deficit disorder, conduct disorder, and a learning disability. His IQ was measured to be in the low normal range.

Bryan said that he rarely went to school so that he could stay at home with his mother. School personnel said that he would come to school "reeking of marijuana," and when confronted by teachers about his behavior, he would curse at them. One teacher said she recalled his being in school only four times during the school year. He was functionally illiterate. The staff at the school believed that he was involved in selling drugs. The psychologist who interviewed him for the court indicated that Bryan was aggressive and displayed little regard for authority figures, his peers, or the law. He had been arrested at least four times before.

At the beginning of the twenty-first century, the population of adolescents in the United States between ten and seventeen years of age was approximately 30 million. The population of youth between fifteen and seventeen years old, the ages of peak antisocial behavior in adolescents, was 9.3 million. At this same time there were approximately 2.3 million arrests made of young people under the age of eighteen for breaking the law. Of these, close to one hundred thousand were for violent crimes including murder, rape, robbery, and aggravated assault. The overall arrest rate for all crimes was approximately 7,400 arrests per 100,000 adolescents. And the rate at which juveniles commit crimes is actually higher than is indicated by their arrest rates.

Adolescent criminal behavior creates an enormous drain on our national resources in terms of the cost of policing and courts and the costs of treatment and/or incarceration. The cost of the wasted lives of these young people is immeasurable, as is the cost in pain and suffering to their victims. We face a problem of epidemic proportions. A physical disorder that affected our coming generation of adults to this extent would certainly be cause for alarm. Yet, our response as a nation to this problem has too often been inadequate, misguided, and not based on the information that has been available for decades to social scientists including psychologists, psychiatrists, and sociologists.

Definitions

From a social or legal point of view, the term *juvenile delinquent* refers to any adolescent who breaks the law. Adolescents, as a group in our society, tend to engage in risk-taking behavior at a higher level than their older contemporaries; they are likely to experiment with drugs, alcohol, and sex in ways that cause great alarm among parents and teachers. The 1997 National Longitudinal Survey of Youth, a self-report survey of adolescents between twelve and sixteen years of age, found that 29 percent reported having engaged in sex, 42 percent reported using cigarettes, 39 percent said they had consumed alcohol, and 21 percent said they had used marijuana. Adolescents take greater physical risks and are involved in automobile accidents at a much higher rate than the rest of the population. Some of this risk-taking behavior involves breaking the law. Most of the offenses are minor, often classified as "status offenses." A status offense relates to breaking a law that is related only to minors, such as underage drinking, truancy, and running away from home. Other minor offenses might include petty larceny, for example shoplifting, or experimentation with drugs. While such behaviors might be indicative of more serious problems, they are more typically self-limiting and tend to stop before the individual reaches adulthood. Labeling all teenagers who are accused of these minor offenses as "delinquents" dilutes the definition of delinquency.

This book is primarily about the adolescents who repeatedly commit serious offenses, and less about those who are guilty of the occasional minor offense or those who may commit only one or two more serious offenses. The distinction between the two types is quite important because there are a number of studies that show these two groups of young people most often have different backgrounds and histories and therefore need to be understood and responded to in very different ways.

Len, a fifteen-year-old boy referred to me by the court, is an example of a more limited offender. Len had stolen an expensive car from the parking lot of a suburban train station. The owner had left the keys in the car. The adolescent took the car for a short time, and when the police found him he was asleep in the car, not far from the station. He had committed a felony, a serious offense, but since this was his first offense, the court put him on probation. Conversations with Len revealed that his mother had recently remarried and had had a new baby with his stepfather. His biological father lived in another state, and was only able to visit Len infrequently. He told me that since the baby was born, his mother had very little time for him. When she came home from work, she went straight to the baby's room, and rarely stopped in his room to see how he was doing. His perceptions were verified when I met with her. She was clearly more involved with other issues in her life, including her appearance, than she was with her adolescent son. Stealing the car was a way for Len to get her attention. I suggested to his mother and stepfather that they try to find a way to spend more time with Len, a suggestion that they were responsive to. Len has since successfully graduated from high school and has not had any further trouble with the law. To put Len in the same category as a Bryan, who has committed a series of assaults and been repeatedly arrested, would blur the definition of delinquency.

A precise definition of delinquency is important for three reasons. First, because it makes communication about delinquent behavior clear. When delinquency is mentioned, it can be assumed that everyone is talking about the same behavior. Second, when research is conducted on the problem of delinquency, the nature of the problem can be agreed upon. Third, it more clearly defines the population that needs help either by altering existing behavior or preventing it.

The *Diagnostic and Statistical Manual,* fourth edition, of the American Psychiatric Association, more commonly referred to as the DSM IV, is a compilation of all of the recognized psychiatric disorders, grouped by category: mood disorders, substance abuse disorders, anxiety disorders, and so forth. Each disorder lists a set of behavioral and other criteria which must be present in the individual to warrant a given diagnosis. The authors of the DSM IV state that "the specified diagnostic criteria for each mental disorder are offered as guidelines for making diagnoses, because it has been demonstrated that the use of such criteria enhances agreement among clinicians and investigators. . . . The purpose of the DSM IV is to provide clear descriptions of diagnostic categories in order to enable clinicians and investigators to diagnose, communicate about, study and treat people with various mental disorders" (American Psychiatric Association, 1994, xxvii).

The DSM IV criteria for what is known as conduct disorder appear in table 1.1. One of the underlying criteria for conduct disorder is that the behavior in question be repetitive and persistent; the child or adolescent has to have exhibited three or more of the behaviors described during a one-year period. These include behaviors that involve aggression (such as initiating fights), destruction of property, deceitfulness, theft (such as shoplifting), or serious violation of rules that apply to minors (such as chronic truancy). The diagnosis of conduct disorder also requires that the clinician specify whether the problem is mild, moderate, or severe. The rating of severe indicates that the child or adolescent has exhibited a large number of the behaviors or that the behaviors exhibited have caused serious harm to the victims.

The large majority of seriously antisocial adolescents would meet the criteria for severe conduct disorder. Also, with the exception of the last category—"serious violation of rules," which includes status offenses—all the criteria involve breaking laws and many involve vio-

Table 1.1. Diagnostic Criteria for Conduct Disorder

Aggression to people and animals
1. often bullies, threatens, or intimidates others
2. often initiates fights
3. has used a weapon that can cause serious physical harm
4. has been physically cruel to people or animals
5. has stolen while confronting a victim
6. has forced someone into sexual activity

Destruction of property
7. arson
8. vandalism

Deceitfulness or theft
9. broken into someone's house or car
10. often lies to obtain benefits or avoid obligations
11. stolen items of value without confronting the victim (e.g., shoplifting)

Serious violation of rules
12. stays out at night without parent's permission
13. runs away from home overnight
14. is often truant from school

In order to meet the criteria for conduct disorder the child or adolescent must have demonstrated at least three or more of these criteria within a twelve-month period. The diagnosis is also modified by the age of onset. *Childhood onset type* requires that at least one criterion be present prior to age ten. *Adolescent onset type* requires that no criteria be present prior to age ten. In addition, the diagnosis is also modified by severity. *Mild:* minimal number of criteria met with little harm to others. *Severe:* many criteria met or considerable harm to others.

Source: Adapted from *Diagnostic and Statistical Manual of Mental Disorders* from American Psychiatric Association, (2000), 90–91.

lence. Len would be defined as a delinquent from a legal point of view, but would not meet the criteria for conduct disorder because his behavior was not repetitive and persistent. Bryan, however, would meet the criteria for both definitions. Society suffers most from adolescents whose antisocial behavior persistently violates criminal laws.

Most children brought to family courts for antisocial behavior meet the criteria for conduct disorder, but not all conduct-disordered adolescents are necessarily delinquents, and some may never come to the attention of the law. A class bully may meet the criteria for conduct disorder but not a social/legal definition of delinquency. And there are instances in which very serious law violators, such as the teenagers who shoot their classmates, may be first-time offenders and so would not meet the criteria for conduct disorder.

The problem with the term *juvenile delinquent* is that it is a legal concept that varies from one state to another; this is why I believe *conduct disorder,* a psychiatric definition, is preferable because it more precisely delineates the group of adolescents that most concerns society. It defines the individual on the basis of his or her behavior regardless of legal involvement, and it is a more consistent definition. Defining these youngsters as conduct-disordered adolescents (CDAs) would provide a more consistent and uniform definition regardless of the legal variations that exist among different states. In addition, the research on conduct disorder suggests that we are dealing with the same population as delinquents in terms of their school histories, family backgrounds, temperaments, and other associated psychiatric disorders, such as attention deficit hyperactivity disorder and borderline personality disorder (see chapters 3 and 4). (For stylistic reasons I will also refer to conduct-disordered adolescents as juvenile delinquents or antisocial youths. However, my underlying meaning is as I have described.)

There are, of course, implications of using a psychiatric, as opposed to a social or legal, definition for antisocial behavior. First, it implies that the behavior is the result of a psychiatric disorder, and therefore that it has a particular etiology. It causes us to focus on not only the social issues involved—the criminal behavior and its consequences—but also on the reasons for this behavior that lie within the adolescent. This is not a new or original way of looking at things. August Aichhorn, who wrote a well-known book on delinquency entitled *Wayward Youth* (1935), stated that the symptoms of delinquent behavior are often confused with its causes. In fact this perception of delinquency as a symptom of a psychological disorder is pervasive throughout the psychological and psychiatric literature on delinquency, though it is less emphasized in sociological and criminal justice theories of delinquent behavior. It raises other issues as well. If society, and that includes the criminal justice system, considers delinquent behavior to be symptomatic of an underlying psychiatric disorder, that requires society to respond to the problem in a way that emphasizes treatment and prevention, rather than just enforcement, punishment, and detention. It also raises the issue of criminal responsibility in young adolescents. Should fifteen year olds diagnosed with a mental disorder be held criminally responsible, if they were unaware they were doing something wrong and/or could not have controlled the impulse to do it? These issues were raised by the founders of the first juvenile court in Chicago over a century ago.

Considering Numbers—Taking Count

How many adolescents commit serious crimes, what kinds of serious crimes do they commit, and how often do they commit them? Unfortunately these are not questions that can be answered with a great deal of accuracy, because a lot of crime is unreported or unresolved (i.e., the perpetrator is never apprehended) or the data are inaccurate for other reasons. However, there are sources of information available that can provide at least approximate answers. Table 1.2 is reproduced from the most recent edition of the Uniform Crime Reports (UCR), a yearly document compiled by the Federal Bureau of Investigation in a publication called *Crime in the United States.* The FBI collects information on arrests from police departments across the country on a voluntary basis and then summarizes the information in various ways. (All police precincts do not necessarily submit information, and in some instances an entire state might not contribute data. Obviously this makes literal comparisons and interpretation impossible.) The summaries consist of the number of arrests made for various crimes and demographic information on the individual arrested, such as age, gender, and race. In addition, the FBI also computes the changes in the arrest rate over time, which makes it possible to examine trends. (Different tables present different demographic breakdowns. I have presented only ten-year trends for age and gender. The complete UCR is available on the internet through the FBI's web site [FBI.Gov].)

The more serious crimes are referred to as index crimes. These are divided into two categories, violent crime and property crime. Violent crimes include murder and non-negligent manslaughter, forcible rape, robbery, and aggravated assault. Nonviolent index crimes include bur-

Table 1.2. Ten-Year Arrest Trends Totals, 1993–2002 [7,596 agencies; 2002 estimated population 175,384,794; 1993 estimated population 157,011,564]

Offense charged	Number of persons arrested								
	Total all ages			Under 18 years of age			18 years of age and over		
	1993	2002	Percent change	1993	2002	Percent change	1993	2002	Percent change
TOTAL[1]	8,581,290	8,413,983	-1.9	1,564,326	1,393,752	-10.9	7,016,964	7,020,231	*
Murder and nonnegligent manslaughter	15,125	8,933	-40.9	2,485	886	-64.3	12,640	8,047	-36.3
Forcible rape	23,509	17,394	-26.0	3,928	2,887	-26.5	19,581	14,507	-25.9
Robbery	96,877	69,405	-28.4	26,505	16,338	-38.4	70,372	53,067	-24.6
Aggravated assault	320,814	299,286	-6.7	49,427	38,082	-23.0	271,387	261,204	-3.8
Burglary	253,751	178,477	-29.7	89,511	54,393	-39.2	164,240	124,084	-24.4
Larceny-theft	959,452	729,825	-23.9	307,926	216,434	-29.7	651,526	513,391	-21.2
Motor vehicle theft	128,552	94,608	-26.4	57,740	28,664	-50.4	70,812	65,944	-6.9
Arson	12,646	10,055	-20.5	6,451	4,957	-23.2	6,195	5,098	-17.7
Violent crime[2]	456,325	395,018	-13.4	82,345	58,193	-29.3	373,980	336,825	-9.9
Property crime[3]	1,354,401	1,012,965	-25.2	461,628	304,448	-34.0	892,773	708,517	-20.6
Crime Index[4]	1,810,726	1,407,983	-22.2	543,973	362,641	-33.3	1,266,753	1,045,342	-17.5
Other assaults	733,037	782,294	+6.7	126,489	143,933	+13.8	606,548	638,361	+5.2
Forgery and counterfeiting	66,364	71,842	+8.3	5,341	3,070	-42.5	61,023	68,772	+12.7
Fraud	218,695	195,925	-10.4	6,449	5,258	-18.5	212,246	190,667	-10.2
Embezzlement	7,910	11,815	+49.4	510	883	+73.1	7,400	10,932	+47.7

Offense								
Stolen property; buying, receiving, possessing	101,613	76,137	−25.1	28,808	15,766	−45.3	72,805	60,371	−17.1
Vandalism	209,095	169,842	−18.8	97,968	65,360	−33.3	111,127	104,482	−6.0
Weapons; carrying, possessing, etc.	175,998	104,418	−40.7	42,530	22,615	−46.8	133,468	81,803	−38.7
Prostitution and commercialized vice	61,811	51,275	−17.0	755	958	+26.9	61,056	50,317	−17.6
Sex offenses (except forcible rape and prostitution)	69,072	59,193	−14.3	13,387	12,198	−8.9	55,685	46,995	−15.6
Drug abuse violations	710,922	974,082	+37.0	73,413	116,781	+59.1	637,509	857,301	+34.5
Gambling	10,348	6,500	−37.2	1,715	1,053	−38.6	8,633	5,447	−36.9
Offenses against the family and children	67,930	79,059	+16.4	3,520	5,208	+48.0	64,410	73,851	+14.7
Driving under the influence	984,141	879,210	−10.7	8,878	12,921	+45.5	975,263	866,289	−11.2
Liquor laws	316,919	385,611	+21.7	75,836	88,574	+16.8	241,083	297,037	+23.2
Drunkenness	509,543	362,979	−28.8	11,705	11,452	−2.2	497,838	351,527	−29.4
Disorderly conduct	483,676	398,728	−17.6	103,747	112,844	+8.8	379,929	285,884	−24.8
Vagrancy	13,581	15,702	+15.6	2,254	1,346	−40.3	11,327	14,356	+26.7
All other offenses (except traffic)	1,834,511	2,209,668	+20.4	221,650	239,171	+7.9	1,612,861	1,970,497	+22.2
Suspicion	6,231	2,252	−63.9	1,239	708	−42.9	4,992	1,544	−69.1
Curfew and loitering law violations	68,042	91,984	+35.2	68,042	91,984	+35.2	—	—	—
Runaways	127,356	79,736	−37.4	127,356	79,736	−37.4	—	—	—

[1] Does not include suspicion.

[2] Violent crimes are offenses of murder, forcible rape, robbery, and aggravated assault.

[3] Property crimes are offenses of burglary, larceny-theft, motor vehicle theft, and arson.

[4] Includes arson.

[5] Less than one-tenth of 1 percent.

Source: Federal Bureau of Investigation, *Crime in the United States* (Washington, DC: U.S. Department of Justice, 2002), 238.

glary, larceny-theft, motor vehicle theft, and arson. Statistics are also kept on arrests for "less serious" crimes such as forgery, carrying a weapon, drug abuse violations, disorderly conduct, curfew violations, driving under the influence, etc. The consequences to the victims of these "less serious" crimes can nonetheless be quite severe.

As I noted earlier, according to UCR the police across the country made approximately 2.3 million arrests of juveniles under the age of eighteen for various offenses in 2001. This represented a 3 percent decrease over the ten-year period between 1992 to 2001. While the majority of all those arrested are adults, about 17 percent of all arrests in 2001 were of adolescents. Figure 1.1 presents a breakdown of arrests of juveniles for various crimes. Young people accounted for 17 percent of all arrests for violent crimes and 30 percent of all arrests for property crimes (McCord, Spatz-Windom, and Crowell, 2001).

While arrest rates for male adolescents decreased by about 6 percent between 1993 and 2002 after several years of dramatic increases, it is interesting to note that the arrest rate of female adolescents has increased by 6.4 percent over the past ten years. In addition, minority youth are disproportionately represented among the population of young offenders. While black youngsters represent 15 percent of the population between the ages of 10 to 17 they account for 26 percent of all arrests of individuals in this age range and 44 percent of the arrests for violent crimes.

While these statistics are useful and interesting, they are also flawed. First, the UCR compiles only the number of reported arrests, not the actual number of different individuals arrested. The same adolescent might be arrested more than one time over the course of a year. Second, an adolescent may commit a number of crimes for which he or she is not arrested. As we know the police do not always get their man or woman. Additionally, many crimes go unreported, so there would not even be an investigation of a crime. Third, as I have noted, reports from police agencies to the FBI are voluntary. It is possible that there may be no data reported from an entire state. Finally, police have discretionary power to make arrests. Possession of a small amount of marijuana that might lead to confiscation of the substance and a warning in one precinct might lead to an arrest in another. And policies change. At any given time, police may be told by the local government to crack

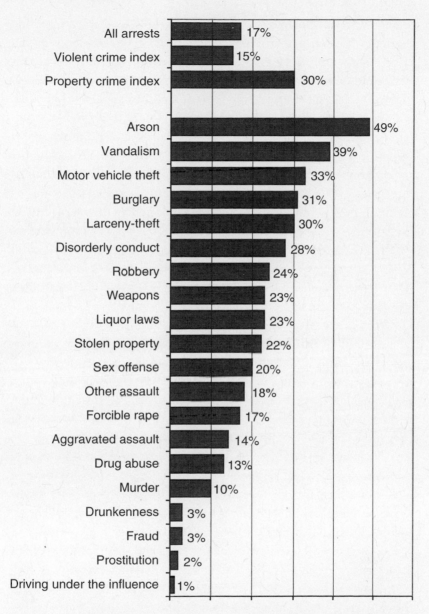

Figure 1.1. Juvenile Proportion of Arrests, by Offense, 2001. *Source:* From H. Snyder, *Juvenile Arrests 2001* (Washington, DC: Office of Juvenile Justice and Delinquency Prevention, 2003).

down on particular types of offenses, so arrest rates may go up while the actual incidence of crime may remain the same. Nonetheless, the UCR represents the best source of information we have regarding trends and demographic breakdowns of persons arrested even though the statistics are not a literal representation of the incidence of juvenile crime.

There are two other sources of data that provide information about the degree of adolescent criminal behavior. These are self-report and victim surveys. Self-report surveys may be administered to teenagers in schools or other settings regarding antisocial behavior, including drug use. Students may be asked whether they have forced someone to have sex with them within the past six months, or whether they have injured someone badly enough that their victim required medical attention. The surveys are administered anonymously. Self-report surveys are likely to indicate criminal behavior for which arrests were not made, and therefore would not be included in FBI statistics. However, the accuracy of the information obtained from these surveys depends entirely on how honest the respondents are. Because the adolescents are being asked about sensitive information, they may not always choose to be honest in their answers.

Since the surveys are also an attempt to get a clear picture of the entire population of juveniles in the country, the adolescents surveyed have to be reasonably representative of all adolescents in the country. This is a statistical sampling problem known as validity. If the sample is not reasonably valid, the conclusions drawn from it are also not valid or accurate. These surveys are not, despite the researcher's best intentions, completely valid. For example, the number of inner-city schools surveyed may be overrepresented. Adolescents who do not attend school regularly are less likely to be included and these are the types of adolescents who are more likely to engage in criminal behavior.

According to the 1997 National Longitudinal Survey of Youth, of the nine thousand youths questioned, who were boys and girls between the ages of twelve and sixteen, 10 percent said they had carried a gun, 5 percent said they belonged to a gang, 28 percent said they had purposely destroyed property, 8 percent stole something worth over $50.00, 7 percent reported selling drugs, 18 percent committed an assault. Generally, when compared to the UCR, these self-report surveys indicate that a much higher proportion of adolescents are involved in delinquent behavior.

A third source of information about juvenile crime comes from surveys of victims. The National Crime Victimization Survey collects information yearly from a sample of 43,000 households. Members of the household over the age of twelve are asked about their experience with crime, whether or not the crime was reported to the police. Information is collected on the types of crime, frequency of victimization, and the victims' perception of the age of the perpetrator. Participants in the survey are questioned every six months over a period of three years. One of the findings of a 1995 survey was that juveniles themselves were a highly victimized group, more so than senior citizens. In close to two-thirds of the instances, the juvenile victims knew the offender, but only about half the incidents were reported to the police or to adults in authority, such as teachers. In the mid-1990s, youth between the ages of twelve and seventeen were victims in about 20 percent of the serious violent crime reported—including rape, robbery, and aggravated assault—and about 26 percent of all the simple assaults. The fact that only half of this crime is reported to the police supports the notion that the UCR underestimates actual occurrences of juvenile crime. (For the most recent data, see the web site of the Office of Juvenile Justice and Delinquency Prevention: www.ojjdp.ncjrs.org.)

One obvious shortcoming of this technique of estimating juvenile crime, based on victim reporting, is that victims are guessing at the age of the perpetrator. It would be quite easy to either overestimate or underestimate the age of the person responsible for the crime, given that such situations generate a high level of emotionality. Further, the survey does not report on crimes against businesses, so theft and robberies directed toward local stores, for example, would not be included.

Another way of looking at changes in frequency and types of juvenile crime is through cohort studies. A cohort is defined as a group of individuals who were born in the same year. By studying a cohort it is possible to look at the behavior of these individuals, antisocial or otherwise, during any particular year or years of their lives. One such study was conducted by Martin Wolfgang, a well-known criminologist, and his colleagues (Tracy, Wolfgang, and Figlio, 1985). They compared a group of adolescents born in 1945 to a group born in 1958. Perhaps one of the most interesting findings to come out of these studies is that a relatively small group of adolescents is responsible for a large amount of juvenile crime. Wolfgang and his colleagues found that 7.5 percent of the groups were recidivists or chronic delinquents. These adolescents were responsible for 61 percent of all offenses. They committed 61 percent of all the homicides, 75 percent of all the rapes, 73 percent of the robberies, and 65 percent of the aggravated assaults.

Similar findings were also obtained in a more recent cohort study, which looked at court records of a group of 150,000 individuals born between 1962 and 1977 in Maricopa County, Arizona (Snyder and Zickmund, 1999). This report also found that the male chronic offenders, in this study defined as someone with four or more court referrals, were responsible for 62 percent of all the male serious referrals and 63 percent of all the male violent referrals. This group constituted about six percent of the total number of males who had at least one court referral. Thus a relatively small group of the male adolescents was responsible for a large amount of adolescent crime in both studies. It is this group of adolescents who create the most serious problem for society and are the most difficult to treat, and they need to be differentiated from the less serious and less chronic adolescent offenders.

Female Delinquency

Female adolescents, in both the cohort studies and other sources of data on antisocial behavior in adolescents, represented a much smaller percentage of the official delinquents. They also tended to be less chronic and less violent when compared to their male counterparts. In the Philadelphia study, males were two and half times more likely to be delinquent than females, and females were only one-third as likely to be chronic offenders. Females are also less likely to commit serious crimes. In the Maricopa County groups, males were almost three times more likely to commit a serious crime than were females.

According to the UCR, in 2001 females represented 28 percent of the total arrests and only 18 percent of the arrests for violent crime. Girls are more likely to be arrested for status offenses, such as running away, than are boys. This may be in part because they are more likely to be sexually abused than are boys. Status offenses accounted for almost 25 percent of the arrests of female adolescents, but only ten percent of the arrests of males. Nonetheless, there is evidence that females are becoming more delinquent and more violent. As I mentioned above, there was a 6.4 percent increase in reported arrests for females between 1993 and 2002, compared to a 10 percent decrease for males over the same period. While male arrests for violent crime decreased by 33 percent during that time period, female violent crime decreased by only 2.4 percent.

A recent event reported in my local newspaper illustrates that females are quite capable of extreme violence: "The 32-year-old counselor, an employee at the residence facility for troubled children since 1996, remained at Westchester Medical Center in Valhalla yesterday. She was taken there early Friday morning [February 8, 2002] after a gang of eight girls allegedly beat her with a telephone, doused her with rubbing alcohol and chlorine bleach, set her afire, cut her hair with scissors and kicked her down two flights of steps. The attack continued for more than an hour, authorities said"(Gorman, 2002, 1A).

The reasons for this change in serious female delinquency are not clear. There are some who suggest that it has to do with changes in the way girls are socialized in our culture. Others believe it may have to do with a lessening in social tolerance for even lesser offenders, leading the police to arrest female adolescents for even minor offenses. In the past these girls might have been released after a warning, or released in the custody of their parents, for the same offenses. Female delinquency has been an area which has not been adequately studied and, in view of the increase in violent female offenders, clearly needs more attention from researchers and practitioners, both in terms of its causes and in terms of developing gender-specific responses to the problem when necessary. (See chapter 3 for a further discussion of conduct-disordered female adolescents.)

Race and Delinquency

While females are underrepresented among the total population of delinquents, black adolescents are overrepresented. In 2002, black adolescents totaled approximately 15 percent of the juvenile population, but according to FBI statistics, they accounted for 50 percent of the arrests for murder and 59 percent of the arrests for robbery. In fact, they accounted for 43 percent of the arrests for violent crimes, nearly three times what would be expected from their numbers in the population data (Federal Bureau of Investigation, 2002). Black youth were also more likely to use firearms in the commission of a homicide than were whites. Additionally, they accounted for a disproportionate number of the juveniles who are put into residential placement, as well as those who are sent to criminal as opposed to family court.

It is important to be aware that minority children and black youth in particular are more often raised in poverty than are white youth. In 2000 black children were 2.5 times more likely to live in poverty than white children (31 percent versus 13 percent). As a result, black children as a group are more likely to be raised in high-crime neighborhoods. They also attend schools in poorer neighborhoods which are less likely to offer the same educational opportunities as found in more affluent areas, and black families disproportionately live under a higher degree of socioeconomic and psychosocial stress. All of these factors contribute to antisocial behavior in adolescence. (See chapter 2 for further discussion of the effects of poverty on behavior.) Furthermore, black youth may be subject to a greater amount of bias within the juvenile justice system. They stand a greater risk of being arrested, being referred to juvenile court, and being placed in a residential facility than their white counterparts. Professor Mathew Johnson, of the John Jay College of Criminal Justice, notes that in New Jersey black and Latino youth are more than three times more likely to be incarcerated than their white counterparts and concludes that there is clear evidence that African American teenagers are subject to discrimination in the juvenile justice system (Johnson 2001). The issue of racial profiling has gained significant attention lately and probably plays a contributory role in the arrest rates of black adolescents (McCord, Spatz-Windom, and Crowell, 2001).

Conclusions

Since definitions often determine how we begin to understand and respond to a problem, I have suggested that the term *juvenile delinquent,* while widely used, is too vague to be of value and emphasizes the legal, as opposed to psychological, issues that are involved. The individuals that create the most difficulty for society are those who would be diagnosed as having a severe conduct disorder. Defining adolescents who frequently break the law as conduct-disordered adolescents shifts the locus of the response from police and courts to psychological and social interventions.

Much of what we know about the extent of delinquency is only an approximation. The official statistics produced by the FBI only report arrest data that is reported to them. Since all crimes do not involve an arrest, these data probably underreport juvenile crime. Other sources of information about juvenile crime, including victim surveys, self-report surveys of adolescents, and data from the juvenile court, also have shortcomings. However, it is reasonable to say that while a very large percentage of adolescents admit to breaking the law, the large majority of these adolescents are not serious offenders; many are never arrested and so never get to court. Of those who are arrested and brought to the attention of the court, most do not return for a second time. Nonetheless, there is a small percentage of adolescents who become chronic and sometimes violent offenders, and they are responsible for about two-thirds of the serious juvenile crime. These youth are much more likely to be male, and a disproportionate number of them are black. It is this small group of adolescents that creates the greatest problem for society. It is important that we begin to understand the ways in which these children come to be who they are and the ways in which we have responded to them up to now.

2

Childhood and Delinquency

I saw ten thousand talkers whose tongues were all broken,
I saw guns and sharp swords, in the hands of young children . . .
And it's a hard rain's a-gonna fall.

Bob Dylan, "A Hard Rain's A-Gonna Fall"

Mark was fifteen when he took part in a car jacking. When the victim resisted, Mark shot him, and as a result the victim was paralyzed below the waist. Mark is an adopted child whose parents both work. He began having difficulties at school in the first grade. Hyperactive and disruptive in class, he was diagnosed as having attention deficit hyperactivity disorder and prescribed Ritalin, a drug commonly used for controlling hyperactivity in children. Failing in school, he eventually stopped attending when he was fourteen.

Mark's parents were divorced. The marriage had been difficult and angry. The father was an alcoholic, and on several occasions Mark had witnessed him being physically abusive to his mother. His mother reported to the court that she always had difficulty dealing with Mark's behavior and his frequent outbursts of temper. She had sought help from a local mental health clinic when he was younger but stopped after a few visits because she felt that he "wasn't making any progress." Mark told the psychologist who was examining him for the court that he had been stealing money from his parents and playing with fire. While his official records are sealed because he is a minor, Mark admitted to committing several minor offenses and a serious assault prior to his arrest. He also stated that he had taken a gun to school on a number of occasions for "protection."

If, instead of being delinquent, Mark had a physical disease and we knew that this disease affected about 6 percent of the children in the United States, we would certainly try to determine the reasons why that disease occurs in children, so that we might be able to prevent it if possible and/or develop a cure for it. Chronic juvenile delinquency is a symptom of a serious developmental disorder that, according to the Surgeon General of the United States, represents a significant public health problem (Satcher, 2001). Understanding the reasons why children become antisocial and responding to those reasons is no less important than understanding why they develop physical diseases and finding ways of preventing it.

Causality in Social Science

When I teach students who are new to psychology, I always begin by telling them that the science of psychology is primarily concerned with two issues. First, accurately and objectively describing behavior and, second, attempting to explain how and why behaviors occur. However, as I will demonstrate, explanations for many behaviors, including antisocial behavior, tend to be complex and multidimensional.

There has been no shortage of theories as to why adolescents become delinquent or adults become criminals. Many of them are common knowledge. For instance, most of us are familiar with the explanation that "poverty breeds crime." To some degree that is true. Poorer neighborhoods do have higher rates of crime and delinquency. In other words, the probability of a delinquent coming from a poor neighborhood is higher than a delinquent coming from a more affluent neighborhood. But poverty alone is not a sufficient explanation, because the large majority of people who live in poor neighborhoods are not criminals and the large majority of adolescents living in poor neighborhoods are not delinquents. In addition, there are certainly delinquent adolescents who do not come from poor neighborhoods. While poverty is often associated with antisocial behavior, poverty alone cannot explain delinquent behavior.

For a long time social scientists tended to look for singular explanations for behaviors. In the nineteenth century an Italian physician by the name of Cesare Lombroso suggested that criminals were less physically developed than other people. He believed that they were evolutionary "throwbacks" and hypothesized that the skulls of criminals differed from those of modern man. They had, he said, larger jaws and higher cheekbones. He believed that criminality was an inborn characteristic. His research was flawed for a number of reasons, not the least of which was his failure to use a control group. Unlike the explanations posited on poverty, which were based on social factors, his explanation for criminal behavior rested on biology (Lambroso-Ferrero, 1972).

Other explanations for antisocial behavior continued to be developed, including the absence of a father in the home, having a low IQ, having a particular type of chromosomal makeup or watching too many violent television programs. Many of these explanations have some merit; others have none. All suffer from the fact that they attempt to explain delinquent behavior based on a single variable. Just as it is true that poverty is associated with juvenile delinquency, it is also true that not having a father living at home or having less than normal intelligence is associated with delinquent behavior. But what is equally true is that most children without fathers or with less than average intellectual ability are not delinquent. Clearly the reasons are more complex.

Behavior (delinquent or otherwise) is the result of a myriad of factors acting in concert. These include biological factors, including genetic and neurological makeup; factors which exist in the individual's immediate environment such as family, friends, neighborhood; and the individual's unique history, for example how they were raised and what successes and failures they experienced in school. It is impossible to separate these factors out. It's like a cake made up of a number of ingredients, none of which can be identified separately after it is baked but each of which makes a necessary contribution to the final product. This makes understanding why any particular child becomes a delinquent quite difficult. To add to the complexity, time has to be taken into account. These causal factors are not static; they may influence behavior in different ways at different points in a person's life. For example, not having a father means different things to a five year old than it does to an infant.

Table 2.1. Risk Factors for Serious Conduct Disorder in Childhood and Adolescence

Problems within the child	**School factors**
Difficult temperament	Poor academic performance
Impulsive behavior	Above normal age for grade
Hyperactive and disruptive behavior	Poor attachment to school
Substance use	Poor educational motivation
Aggression	Poorly functioning school
Early-onset disruptive behavior	**Peer factors**
Withdrawn behavior	Delinquent siblings or peers
Low intelligence	Rejection by peers
Lead toxicity	**Neighborhood factors**
Family factors	Economically disadvantaged
Parental antisocial behavior	neighborhood
Parental substance abuse	Availability of weapons
Poor parental supervision, discipline,	Violence in the media
communication	
Poor parent-child relationship	
Physical or sexual abuse	
Maternal depression	
Mother smoking during pregnancy	
Teenage motherhood	
Parents disagree on child discipline	
Single parenthood	
Large family	
Low socioeconomic status	
Unemployment	
Poorly educated mother	
Poor supervision of access to weapons	

Source: Adapted from R. Loeber and D. P. Farrington (2000). Young children who commit crime: Epidemiology, developmental origins, risk factors, early interventions and policy implications. *Development and Psychopathology,* 12, 749.

Variables that are associated or correlated with delinquency are called risk factors. These would include such things as gender, since the ratio of serious male delinquents to serious female delinquents is a about ten to one. From a probabilistic perspective, being a male puts a child at greater risk for becoming delinquent than being female. Other risk factors include poverty, school failure, and having an attention deficit disorder. The list of risk factors is in fact quite long. Table 2.1

shows the most widely studied risk factors associated with conduct disorder in juveniles. Some contribute more heavily than others, but all have been shown to have some relationship to antisocial behavior in children and adolescents.

Risk factors are typically determined or discovered through either longitudinal studies or retrospective studies. In longitudinal studies a group of children is followed over a period of time, say between the ages of four and twenty. Data is collected periodically from various sources including parents, teachers, peers, and the children themselves, about those variables—for example, discipline or behavior in school—that the researchers believe are relevant to a delinquent outcome. These variables are then correlated with the degree of antisocial behavior exhibited by the children. Such studies, if well designed, can yield significant amounts of useful information. One example of this type of research is the Pittsburgh Youth Study (Loeber, Stouthamer-Loeber, Farrington, Lahey, Keenan, and White, 2002). The authors sampled approximately fifteen hundred boys from the first, fourth, and seventh grades from an inner city area in Pittsburgh. The study, which started in 1987, was designed to examine the development of antisocial behavior from childhood and early adolescence through early adulthood. Data has been collected on such variables as delinquency, substance abuse, psychopathology, family discipline and supervision, neighborhood demographics, etc. The study, which is now in its sixteenth year, has resulted in a wealth of data on the development of delinquent behavior. The drawbacks of such studies is that they obviously take a long time (most will run at least ten years), they are expensive, and the children who participate in the studies may move or drop out of the study for a variety of reasons.

Another way of collecting information about risk factors is to collect information regarding relevant variables from a known group of juvenile delinquents and compare them to a comparable group of nondelinquents. For example, information could be collected about family substance abuse from a group of teenagers living in a poor neighborhood in order to determine the degree to which parental substance abuse is associated with delinquency. Note that by comparing groups of children who live in poor neighborhoods we are eliminating (or controlling for) poverty as a relevant variable. These studies are easier to conduct and less costly. However, they do not give as clear a sense of changes in the child's behavior over time. While it is possible to ask the parent about what the child's behavior was like ten years ago, it's not likely to produce as accurate a picture as asking what the child's behavior has been like over the past week, which is possible in a longitudinal study. Sometimes, however, it is possible to obtain school or medical records of the child's or family's history and then correlate it with the adolescent's current behavior. It is largely through these two types of studies that information on risk factors is accumulated.

Child psychologists Alan Kazdin and Jerome Kagan (1994) have pointed out that risk factors typically operate in clusters and are frequently correlated with each other. For example, poverty, parental neglect, and poor academic performance often occur together. They also expressed concern that studies often will offer only a single reason for a particular outcome, ignoring other important factors. Here is an example of one such study. In the *New York Times,* on March 29, 2002, there was a report on a study that suggested that adolescents who watch more than an hour of television per day were more likely to commit violent crimes and generally behave more aggressively. This study differed from earlier studies on the relationship between television and violent behavior in that it focused on the viewing habits of adolescents instead of children and it wasn't restricted to watching violent television programs. The relationship between TV and violence held up for boys but not for girls (Kolata, 2002, A25). While this information is interesting, and certainly lots of adolescents watch too much television, they do not all become violent. More importantly it doesn't say why adolescents who watch more than seven hours of television per week are more likely to become violent.

There are other characteristics associated with risk factors that are important to bear in mind. Risk only implies likelihood, not certainty. A person who is overweight and doesn't exercise has a greater probability of suffering a heart attack than someone of normal weight who exercises regularly. However, some sedentary overweight people live long lives and many, albeit many fewer, trim exercisers die from heart attacks.

While risk factors are correlated with outcomes, they don't tell us how the resulting behavior is created. Knowing that not having a father is associated with becoming delinquent doesn't explain how not having a father contributes to delinquency. It might be that it is because boys need adequate role models. Not having a father might contribute because intact families have higher income levels, meaning that the child's mother may not have to work long hours and may be able to spend more time with her child. It isn't necessarily not having a father, per se, that causes children to become delinquent, but rather it is not having an adequate role model and/or adequate financial resources. Many delinquents have fathers living at home and in these instances it may be that having no father is better than having an abusive one. Even when a study shows that one particular variable is related to delinquency, it doesn't necessarily mean that that particular variable causes delinquency, only that it is associated or correlated with it. A child might have several risk factors that are associated with delinquent behavior and still not become a delinquent (Kazdin and Kagan, 1994). It is also important to be able to describe the process by which the factor, or factors, create the outcome that concerns us. For example *how* does neglect, in combination with other factors, lead to delinquent behavior?

What is needed is a framework that can be used to integrate all of these variables and at the same time allow us to look at the process by which outcomes are created. One field of study which takes these factors into account and examines the process over time is developmental psychology. This approach provides explanations of how behavior unfolds over the course of life, taking into account the various biological and environmental forces that contribute to those outcomes. It is an eclectic approach, not wedded to any particular theory but rather providing a paradigm for integrating them. (This is not to say that developmental psychologists do not have a particular theoretical bent. Typically they do. Often they will focus on one particular aspect of development, as in Piaget's theory of cognitive development.) However, as an overall conceptual framework, I believe that it is the best way of conceptualizing how children eventually become delinquent.

Consistent with the concerns about understanding how a risk factor operates is the approach taken by Uri Bronfenbrenner, a child psychologist from Cornell University (Bronfenbrenner, 1979). Bronfenbrenner felt that development could be understood only in the context of the environment in which it occurred. His formula for development was $Dt = tp(E)$. This states that the development of the child (D) at any given time (t) is a function of the person (p), which includes that individual's biological makeup or temperament as well as his or her history of interacting with the particular environment (E).

Bronfenbrenner was critical of what he called the "social address" model, which ascribed causality only to environmental factors, without taking the characteristics of the individual into account. He felt that it was important to describe the way in which the environment and the individual interact to produce a particular outcome. For example, children with low birth weights typically have more problematical childhoods than children with normal birth weights. In this example birth weight, a biological variable, is a risk factor. However, in families where mothers, an environmental variable, pay more attention to the low-birth-rate babies, the outcome for those babies is the same as for the normal-birth-rate babies. Thus, understanding the interaction between the environment (E), that is, the behavior of the baby's mother, and the characteristics of the baby (p) provides us with a more accurate picture of how a risk factor operates in context. To add to the complexity, the child influences and changes his environment just as he is influenced and changed by his environment. For example, a hyperactive child is more likely to generate negative responses from his environment than a more even-tempered child. The negative responses from the environment will, in turn, influence his future behavior.

The Sandbox Mugging

If we were sitting in a playground watching mothers and their young children, we might observe the following scene. Two toddlers are playing in the sandbox. Danny is playing with a dump truck; Sean is playing with a pail and shovel. Growing tired of the dump truck, Danny decides that he would rather be playing with Sean's pail and shovel, so he attempts to take it from Sean, without asking his permission. Sean, who is not ready to give up on the pail and shovel, resists Danny's attempt to take the toy from him. Danny becomes more forceful and hits Sean over the head with his dump truck, causing Sean to cry, at which point Danny takes the pail and shovel away from Sean. Two "crimes" have been committed: aggravated assault and robbery. The police are not called. The toddlers' mothers spring into action instead.

Had these two toddlers been fifteen years older, and had Danny attempted to forcefully remove a bicycle from Sean and then hit him with a baseball bat when he resisted, the police would be called. It is interesting to note that though the behaviors of both the toddlers and the teenagers are the same, in the case of the toddlers, mothers are called to respond and in the case of the teenagers the police are called. While we don't condone Danny's behavior, we don't consider it a crime either, because at the age of two and a half Danny doesn't know any better and would have a very hard time controlling his impulse to take the toy even if he did. However, we expect Danny the teenager to know and behave better. Danny the teenager is a delinquent; Danny the toddler is not, even though *they have engaged in the same behavior.* Age and time matter. Teenage Danny should have learned not to take what doesn't belong to him and not to hit others.

Sigmund Freud suggested that children are born with aggressive and sexual instincts and the tendency to gratify those instincts without much regard for reality or the needs of others. He referred to the self-gratifying tendency as the pleasure principle. This was an idea that did not sit well with many of his contemporaries, who believed that children, although conceived in sin, were born innocent. They felt that the minds of children were blank screens on which the rules of culture and civilization could be written and that children's behavior was determined entirely by the environment. There is much of the nature-versus-nurture, or heredity-versus-environment, debate in this disagreement between Freud and his contemporaries. Freud was suggesting that biological instincts, which lead to self-serving behaviors, such as forcibly taking pails and shovels, were part of our inherent makeup, just as they were in animals—a concept he no doubt derived in part from Darwin. While he wasn't suggesting that we were born delinquent, he was suggesting that we were born with the propensity to become that way. There were those who strenuously objected to, and still object to, the idea that individuals are born with propensities, particularly antisocial ones, or ones that suggest that all of us are not born with an equal potential. Anthropologists and sociologists in particular emphasize the importance of the environment in determining human behavior. The well-known anthropologist Margaret Mead went to great lengths to prove that the experience of adolescence wasn't universal but rather was based on a cultural context (Mead, 1950). Being born into a musical family alone didn't make W. A. Mozart the musical genius he was; he must have had considerable inherent talent. Yet, had Mozart been born into an impoverished environment where he had no opportunity to hear music, he might never have become the famous composer he was. Genetic potential and the environment operate together to produce behavior, or as in Mozart's case great music.

Let's then assume that toddler Danny's instincts "drove him" to forcibly take the pail and shovel from little Sean. We can see that if this behavior continues unabated, teenage Danny will become a delinquent. His behavior needs to be transformed, so that it becomes moral, empathetic, and civilized. Danny needs to become socialized. Freud suggested that this depended on the development of an ego (the executive, reality-based part of his model of the mind), and a superego (that part of the mind which is identified with morality). However one conceives of the transformation, ultimately, the child needs to learn to control his impulses and learn to behave in a way that is consistent with the conventions of society, as opposed to his own self-serving needs. The failure of this transformation leads to delinquent behavior in adolescence. Therefore, understanding the development of delinquent behavior requires a comprehension of how that transformation to socialized behavior occurs, as well as what factors lead to the failure of the child to become a socialized being.

Let's return to the "scene of the crime," the sandbox, and consider what happens after Danny hits Sean and takes his pail and shovel. Both Danny's and Sean's mothers will need to respond to the altercation. Sean's mother needs to soothe and calm her injured child. Danny's mother's task is more complex, since she needs to convey to Danny that what he did was wrong. First she must indicate to Danny that the pail and shovel belong to Sean and that he cannot play with them without Sean's permission, and secondly that it is wrong to hit someone else. She might require Danny to make amends by returning the pail and shovel and apologizing. Danny might not think this is a very good idea and resist, but it is nonetheless a lesson he has to learn if he is to become socialized.

It is important to understand the ways in which this interaction between Danny and his mother occurs. There are many possible variations, which can lead to quite different outcomes. The variations depend, in Bronfenbrenner's schema, upon Danny's (p) characteristics, such as his temperament, the history of the relationship between him and his mother (E), and the unique mix that results from this interaction.

In the best of all possible worlds, Danny's mother would be concerned about her son's behavior but at the same time understand that he is not yet capable of comprehending the difference between right and wrong. She might take the pail and shovel away from Danny, give it back to Sean, and in a firm but loving way that communicated her understanding of how much he wanted to play with the pail and shovel, let him know that he couldn't have it unless Sean let him play with it. Furthermore, she would let him know that he shouldn't hit other children, even if he felt angry at them. This lesson would need to be repeated a number of times in different situations until Danny "got it." For his part Danny would, under normal circumstances, acquiesce because he wants to please his mother, he doesn't want her to be angry at him, and because she is more powerful than he is. Eventually this and other experiences under similar circumstances should lead Danny to ask if he could have a turn playing with the pail and shovel, as opposed to just grabbing it and fighting over it. This might take some time, but by the time Danny is ready for preschool, at around four years old, he should have begun to grasp and implement the concept.

This ideal outcome is predicated on a "normal" child and a "normal" mother. To the degree that either or both of them are not "normal" the outcome will be less than optimal. Normal is not easily defined in psychology, nor is it absolute. It is, in fact, a term which is relative to the observer and setting in which the observation is made. What constitutes normal behavior in one culture or subculture might not be considered normal in another, and what constitutes normal behavior at one period of time might not constitute normal behavior in another. For example, corporal punishment of children was considered to be a "normal," even desirable, response to children's misbehavior a hundred years ago, whereas today it is considered to be not only inappropriate but also abusive. What constitutes "normal" aggression in a

two year old isn't considered at all normal in a sixteen year old. Nonetheless, we can think about a normal environment as one which will
produce a reasonably good outcome for the child, understanding that
there is latitude in what constitutes a "good outcome"(Hartman, 1958).
By normal in this situation I am referring to an understanding that
Danny and his mother both have the biological and psychological ca-
pacity to respond to the psychosocial realities regarding reasonable behavior. Significant deviations from the norm in either Danny or his
mother or the nature of the interactions which lead to less than reasonable outcomes are what I have referred to as risk factors. Whether or
not risk factors in early childhood will ultimately lead to delinquent
behavior in adolescence depends upon numerous other variables, such
as later life experiences as well as protective factors, which I will discuss
further on. Nonetheless, it is possible to describe what risk factors existed in the lives of children who later go on to exhibit behavior problems.

Inherent Risk Factors in Infancy and Early Childhood

Despite the fact that I am now going to address individual risk factors,
it is important to remember that these variables operate in the context
of, or in concert with, other variables existing within the child and his
or her environment. While they do not operate in isolation, they can
only be discussed one at a time.

Basic to the development of any living organism is its genetic
makeup. Many of us learned in high school biology how to determine
from a Mendelian chart the possible eye colors (phenotype) of the
child of a blue-eyed mother and a brown-eyed father which constitutes
its genetic makeup (genotype). These genetic mechanisms are well established and accepted. We accept that in order for normal physical development to occur, the individual needs to have a normal genetic
makeup. We can readily accept the fact that a woman whose mother
had breast cancer is at greater risk for developing breast cancer than a
woman with no history of breast cancer in her family.

Less accepted by many is the role that genes play in behavior. We
are less comfortable about thinking about our behavioral predispositions, our personal strengths and weaknesses, as in part being deter-

mined at the moment of our conception. This is particularly true when it comes to thinking about negative behaviors, for example our tendency to become unreasonably angry or to be excessively shy. Furthermore, we don't like thinking about one person as being "genetically superior" to another. It raises specters of racism and Nazi visions of a super race, and, after all, we live in country based on the premise that "all men [and women] are created equal."

The role that genes play in determining behavior is confounded by the fact that development occurs within the context of an environment over the course of time. In order for "normal genes" to express themselves in a "normal" way, there needs to be a "normal" environment. It is much easier to accept deviant behavior as resulting from a "deviant" environment because the environment is not an inherent part of the individual, and he or she was not predestined to behave in any particular way. We are more comfortable believing that we can change the problematic behavior by altering the external circumstances—by improving the neighborhood, school, and/or family—and many interventions are based on that assumption.

There is no such thing as a gene for delinquency, but there is evidence that genes influence temperament. The tendency to be shy or uninhibited or fearless or cautious has at least a partial genetic basis. Temperamental dispositions may ultimately increase the likelihood that under certain circumstances a child may behave aggressively or antisocially. A study conducted in 1996 evaluated children at approximately two years of age and then again when they were thirteen. Children who were described as extremely uninhibited at two were much more likely than those who were described as inhibited to exhibit signs of delinquent and aggressive behavior at age thirteen (Schwartz, Snidman, and Kagan, 1996).

Since both genes and the environment play important roles in determining behavior, social scientists need to have research designs that control for the effects of the environment, while looking at variations in genetic makeup. One such technique for conducting research on the role genetic factors play in behavior is to compare the behavioral similarities or dissimilarities of identical, versus fraternal, twins. The results are reported in terms of concordance rates. A high concordance rate means that there is a high probability that the same trait shows up in both members of a biological pair, such as identical twins; a low concordance rate means that the similarity is no different from what would be found in any two members of the general population. The idea behind comparing sets of identical and fraternal twins is that both types of twins have similar environmental experiences, but only the identical twins have the same genetic makeup. Therefore *some* of the behavioral similarity that exists in identical twins that does not exist in fraternal twins can be attributed to the role of the genetic makeup. A study of 759 twin pairs found that temperamental characteristics such as high levels of emotionality are more likely to be exhibited in both members of identical twins as opposed to fraternal twins. High levels of emotionality at age seven were associated with higher levels of delinquency at age seventeen (Gjone and Stevenson, 1997). Other studies comparing identical and fraternal studies have found that the concordance rate for antisocial behavior is higher among pairs of identical twins (Gottesman, Goldsmith, and Carey, 1997; Eley, 1997).

Another way of looking at the role of genetics is in adoption studies. These are typically conducted in Scandinavian countries, where they keep particularly good records. Looking at court records as a reflection of antisocial behavior, it is possible to compare the court contacts of children who were adopted, either at birth or shortly after birth, with the court records of both their adopted and biological parents. If the records of the children are more similar to their adopted parents' than to their biological parents', then theoretically this reflects an environmental influence. If, however, their court records are more similar to their biological parents' then presumably this reflects a biological influence.

S. A. Mednick and his colleagues analyzed the records of over fourteen thousand male and female adoptees registered in Denmark between 1927 and 1947 as well as more than sixty-five thousand court convictions of the adoptees and their biological, as well as adoptive, parents. The results indicated that the court records of the adopted children more closely resembled those of their biological parents than their adoptive parents, despite the fact that they were adopted shortly after birth, thus lending support to the role of genetic factors in the determination of antisocial behavior (Mednick, Gabrielli, and Hutchings, 1984).

While there is support for the idea that an individual's pedigree plays a role in behavior, it is important to remember that though genes may predispose people to certain behavior problems they do not by themselves determine the behavior. Children develop in an environment, which determines how any particular behavioral predisposition unfolds. An aggressive temperament in one environment may result in an antisocial adolescent, but that same temperament in another environment may result into a highly competitive but well-socialized athlete instead.

Nonetheless, children with a biological parent with a childhood history of conduct disorder or criminal behavior are at greater risk for manifesting antisocial behavior themselves. Children with an alcoholic parent are at greater risk for becoming alcohol abusers, and children with a schizophrenic parent are at greater risk for becoming schizophrenic. However, in the case of juvenile delinquency, it is less clear exactly what is inherited. It may be an aggressive temperament, it may reflect an inability to readily learn or accept social values from the environment, or it may reflect an increased need for sensation seeking. Exactly which particular personality traits are inherited and how they then interact with the child's environment over time is less clear than the final outcome of delinquent behavior. Also possible is the likelihood that some children will become delinquent and not have these genetic predispositions. Much of the confusion and debate over what causes delinquency lies in understanding the difference between direct cause and effect relationships, which implies an understanding of the process by which A causes B to happen, and a risk factor (such as a child's genetic makeup), which only relates to the increased likelihood that a particular set of behaviors will appear. This in fact holds true for all the other risk factors as well, whether they lie within the individual, as in the case of pedigree, or in their environment, as does family or neighborhood.

Studies that look at the interaction between genes and environment can be very illuminating. Avshalom Caspi of the Institute of Psychiatry at King's College in London and his colleagues compared a group of boys with a genetic deficiency in the ability to produce a neurotransmitter known as monoamine oxidase A to a group without this genetic defect. Previous research had indicated that a deficiency in this neurotransmitter was associated with aggressive behavior in animals and humans. (Neurotransmitters are the chemicals in the nervous system by which neurons or nerve cells communicate with each other, either by stimulating or inhibiting adjacent neurons.) Within a subgroup of boys who had been maltreated as children, those with the genetic deficit were significantly more likely to exhibit antisocial behavior than those without the genetic deficit. It was the interaction of both the genetic deficiency *and* the experience of being maltreated that resulted in the antisocial behavior as opposed to just one or the other alone (Caspi, McClay, Moffit, Mill, Martin, Taylor, and Poulton, 2002).

Another risk factor inherent in the individual which has been associated with a delinquent outcome is neurological makeup. Many children and adolescents with conduct disorder show varying degrees of neurological impairment, which can result in deficits in impulse control. While some areas of the brain are involved in activation—for example, reaching out for something—other areas are involved in inhibition—not reaching out for something when it is inappropriate to do so. It might not be appropriate because it is dangerous (don't touch the stove because it is hot), or it might be inappropriate for other reasons (don't eat the cookies on the table because we are going to have dinner in ten minutes). In either case, the desire to reach out needs to be inhibited for the child to survive in the world. In the former case physical harm will result: the child will get burned; in the latter, negative social consequences will result: the child's mother will get angry and he or she will get punished.

There is evidence that many children who develop behavior problems have neurological deficits in those areas of the brain, particularly the prefrontal cortex, that control inhibitions (Gorenstein, 1990; Teichner and Golden, 2002). A deficit of this type would make it difficult for our sandbox mugger, Danny, to benefit from his mother's attempts to teach him that taking toys that don't belong to him is wrong. He may understand the concept but be unable to implement it. Anyone who has been on a diet and has tried to control the impulse to eat can appreciate the nature of this difficulty. It is in part about conflict, action versus inhibition. Neurological difficulties are frequently associated with problems in prenatal development. Maternal drug and alcohol abuse, as well as failure to obtain adequate medical care during pregnancy, are often cited as reasons.

Further support for the idea that neurological problems are involved is the fact that children who are diagnosed with conduct disorder are also frequently diagnosed with attention deficit hyperactivity disorder (ADHD). Children with ADHD have difficulty focusing on assigned tasks or just sitting quietly, clearly an instance of a failure of neurological inhibition. These children are often prescribed methylphenidate (Ritalin). This medication is paradoxically a stimulant which activates inhibitory areas of the brain, resulting in reduced hyperactive behavior.

Another consistent finding over time is that adolescent delinquents have, on average, lower IQs than the rest of the population. A large number of studies have consistently found a strong relationship between low IQ scores (particularly low verbal ability) and conduct disorder in children and adolescents (Farrington, 1996). This type of deficit could contribute to delinquent behavior through a decreased ability to function academically, leading the child to feel frustrated and marginalized.

Gender is another important inherent factor in predisposing a child to behavior problems. Just as boys are much more likely to be involved in delinquency than girls, problem behaviors in younger children are more common in boys. Boys are three to four times more likely to be diagnosed with conduct disorder than girls (Zoccolillo, 1993). They are also more likely to be diagnosed with attention deficit disorder, more likely to be stutterers, and more likely to have learning disabilities. It is difficult to say whether this is due to the fact that boys are acculturated to be more aggressive, which they typically are, or whether the aggressive behavior results from the biological differences that exist between boys and girls.

It is most important to bear in mind that any of the inherent biological factors I have discussed do not predestine any child to a childhood or adolescence or adult life of antisocial behavior. These factors do predispose the child to behave in certain ways (e.g., be more outgoing, more emotional, more aggressive), which in turn generates different types of responses in the environment. It is ultimately the interaction of the biological predispositions of the child and his or her environment which will determine whether or not the child becomes antisocial. However, children with more emotional or more aggressive temperaments are more likely to generate more negative responses from their caretakers and teachers, which in turn will exacerbate their aggressive behavior.

Environmental Factors: The Family

All of the inherent factors I have mentioned above will operate differently in different environmental contexts. The child's environment does not remain constant, and the nature of the environment changes for the child as he or she ages. The environment of a very young child is largely established by the child's caretakers, whereas for a child of six or older it is also established by the school the child attends and his or her peers, in addition to the child's family. The effects of the environment on the child can either be direct, as in the case of the interaction between mother and child, or teacher and child, or they can be indirect, as in the case of the neighborhood in which the child lives or his or her socioeconomic circumstances. (Bronfenbrenner referred to the former as micro environments and the latter, those that indirectly affect the child, as exo environments. This distinction becomes important when thinking about interventions [see chapters 4 and 5]). Environments which fail to meet the changing needs of the growing child often result in problems in development. The needs of a two year old are considerably different from those of a six year old.

Countless numbers of studies have implicated problems within the child's family as being responsible for problem behaviors in the child. In infancy and early childhood the primary caretaker is typically the mother or mother surrogate, although with increased numbers of mothers working some form of daycare is becoming more common. Under normal circumstances a bond is formed between the mother and the child. The nature of this bond, along with the importance of early relationships, has been studied extensively (Bowlby, 1969).

Children who have comfortable relationships with their mothers are said to be securely attached. Most children (about two-thirds of all children) have this type of relationship. The other third have relationships that are insecure and are described as anxious attachments. In ex-

perimental situations they show different patterns of behavior than securely attached children. They may cling excessively to their mothers,
be indifferent to them, or may be resistant to being comforted by
them.

Studies in this area have consistently found that children who do
not feel secure in the presence of their mothers are more likely to exhibit behavior problems early in life, both at home and in preschool
settings. Often mothers of such children are likely to have serious
problems of their own, and so are unable to provide their children with
an emotionally secure environment. There are some instances in which
the child, for reasons of temperament or severe developmental disorder, cannot absorb or effectively make use of his mother's care taking,
or the mother may need to be separated for an extended period of time
because of illness or other reasons, but frequently attachment problems relate to behavior of the mother. The mother has to ensure that
the infant and young child is contained in a "normal" emotional environment. Any number of factors may make this difficult, including alcohol or drug abuse, mental illness or the stresses associated with
poverty. Whatever the reasons, her inability to provide emotional security for her child frequently leads to behavior problems from a very
early age. A study conducted at the University of Minnesota looked at
the relationship between the nature of children's attachment to their
mothers at twelve and eighteen months, and their behavior in preschool when they were four and a half to five years old. Children with
anxious, insecure relationships with their mothers were described by
their preschool teachers as more hostile and impulsive and having
poorer social skills. The mothers of the children with behavior problems reported feeling more confused, disorganized, and anxious than
the mothers of children who did not have behavior problems (Erick-
son, Sroufe, and Egeland, 1985).

If we put ourselves back into the playground with Danny and his
mother we could readily see that if Danny's mom was "high," or very
worried about how she was going to get money for rent, that her ca-
pacity to teach him that very important lesson about not taking what
doesn't belong to him and not hitting other children would be significantly diminished. Being disciplined by a parent is fundamentally
learning in an intimate and emotional context. The parent is the

teacher and the child is the pupil. This understood, it should not come as a surprise that the way in which the child is disciplined impacts how the child is socialized, what he or she learns about what is right and what is wrong, and thus how the child behaves. Harsh, inconsistent, or absent discipline has been found to be associated with troublesome behavior (Wasserman, Miller, Pinner, and Jaramillo, 1996). If Danny's mother physically punished him for taking the toy from his playmate, particularly if this were his mother's typical way of disciplining him, he would more likely be concerned with protecting himself from his mother's anger than paying attention to the lesson she was trying to teach. In addition, she would be modeling just the kind of behavior she wants to prevent. Learning cannot take place in a highly emotional context such as is created when harsh physical punishment is applied.

A recent study conducted by Seth Pollak at the University of Wisconsin found that nine-year-old children who had been physically abused were much more sensitive to facial expressions of anger presented to them on a computer screen than were children who were not abused (Pollak, 2003). From an adaptive point of view this makes sense, since being highly sensitive to angry expressions might allow the child to avoid physical punishment. On the other hand, being overly sensitive to anger also creates the tendency to attribute anger or hostility in others when none is intended. A series of studies conducted by Kenneth Dodge (1991) found that antisocial children perceived hostility in others more frequently than children who were less aggressive. Perceiving a hostile intent, even when none is meant, is much more likely to generate a hostile or aggressive response.

If for whatever reason Danny's mother did not intervene at all, nothing would be learned, because Danny wouldn't get any feedback on his behavior. If she responded inconsistently to Danny's behavior, punishing him some of the time but ignoring the behavior at others, he would also have a difficult time learning what the right thing to do would be. Discipline, or how parents teach their children right from wrong and get them to do what is necessary such as homework, chores, etc. is extremely important. In a large-scale review study of predictors of antisocial behavior, parental management techniques were found to be the most significant (Loeber and Dishion, 1983). This has been known for quite some time. In a 1949 article the British child psychiatrist Kate Friedlander wrote: "During the first three years of life, a process of education takes place which is more far-reaching than any other educational effort later on. . . . Owing to the child's absolute dependence on the mother and the strong emotional tie which unites them, the mother's demands [for age-appropriate behavior] are fulfilled without undue stress although each of them imposes a frustration" (Friedlander, 1949, 206). She also noted that "any factor which interferes with the establishment of a firm mother-child relationship and with consistent handling . . . will hinder this process."

One often cited parental management problem is referred to as coercive family interactions. In this type of interaction the child's negative behavior is reinforced, as a result of inconsistent responding on the part of the parent—scolding or punishing the child on one occasion and ignoring the behavior on another occasion. The result is that most interactions between the parent and the child are centered upon negative behavior and the child is rarely praised for positive behavior.

As noted by Friedlander and other more recent researchers, problems in discipline very often are reflections of problems the parents may have themselves. Parents of conduct-disordered children often have problems with drugs or alcohol, depression, or serious psychiatric disorders. They may have experienced poor parenting themselves and have no models on which to base more adequate parenting techniques. The psychologist Harry Harlow, famous for his studies with rhesus monkeys on "mother love," found that female rhesus monkeys deliberately raised without mothers made bad mothers themselves. When they had their own babies they often abused or in some instances tried to kill their offspring. The reality is that children are essentially captive audiences. They cannot, for the most part, alter their parents' behavior. The best they can do is fight back, withdraw, or take their anger and frustration out on others.

The child's family environment is not only made up by how the family interacts but also by how it is constituted—most significantly who the primary caretakers are and the number of children in the family. Numerous studies have pointed to broken families as being related to behavior problems (Farrington and Loeber, 1999). Broken families typically are the result of marital discord preceding the breakup. It often seems that it is as much the exposure to discord, quarreling, and in more extreme instances family violence that impacts the child as it is the actual separation. Also parents who are constantly fighting with each other are under considerably more stress and thus are less able to have a reasonable relationship with their children. The absence of a father can affect children in different ways. Many children are left financially less well off; mothers are under greater stress; there is an absence of a male role model. On the other hand, a child may be better off fatherless than with an alcoholic, abusive father. Family size also has an effect on behavior problems by increasing parental stress, straining financial resources, and allowing parents less time to spend with each child. It has been found that children raised in families of four or more children are at higher risk for delinquency (Farrington and Loeber, 1999).

Socioeconomic Factors

Yet another frequently studied environmental factor is the effect of poverty on children. Poverty has consistently been shown to be associated with antisocial and criminal behavior. In a recent article entitled "The Environment of Childhood Poverty" (2004), Gary Evans of Cornell University identified a large number of psychological and physical stressors that exist in the social and physical environment of children living in poverty. He notes that low-income children are exposed to more violence, family disruption, and separation from their families than their middle-class contemporaries. They are more likely to be exposed to aggressive peers. Their parents are more likely to use harsher discipline and are less likely to be responsive to them and display less warmth. Parents of poor children speak less often to their children and read to them less. In fairness to the parents, they are likely to experience considerably more day-to-day stress themselves compared to middle-class parents and are less likely to have experienced adequate parenting themselves. The teachers of poor children are less likely to be qualified, and there is greater teacher turnover and more student absenteeism in the schools of poor children.

The physical environment of poor children is also harsher. They are exposed to more toxins. For example, they are four times more likely to suffer from unsafe levels of lead in their bodies. They are also more often exposed to airborne pollution, pesticides, and parental smoking. Their housing is less adequate, as are the physical qualities of their schools. The neighborhoods they live in have higher crime rates. Evans points out that it is the cumulative exposure to these risk factors which endangers these children. They are significantly more likely to be exposed to multiple social and physical risk factors than are middle-class children. Many of these risk factors have been shown to be either directly or indirectly associated with antisocial behavior. Vonnie McLoyd (1998) of Duke University notes that chronic poverty has negative effects on IQ, school performance, and emotional development. Many of the psychosocial and physical risk factors I have described in this chapter are found in abundance within the lives of poor children. It makes it difficult to fault them for turning out the way they do.

Support for the assumption that poverty plays a significant role in behavior disorders in children comes from a recent study by E. Jane Costello and her colleagues at the Duke University School of Medicine (Costello, Compton, Keeler, and Angold, 2003). These researchers conducted a longitudinal study of psychiatric disorders among 1,420 rural children in western North Carolina. One-quarter of the children were Native Americans. Psychiatric symptoms, including depression and anxiety disorders as well as behavior disorders, were present at a significantly higher rate among children living below the poverty line. Unexpectedly, in the midst of the study, a gambling casino opened on the American Indian reservation, increasing the income of 14 percent of the Native American families above the poverty level. Costello and her colleagues found that there was a significant *decrease* in the rates of behavioral problems (conduct disorder and oppositional defiant disorder) among the children whose family income increased. Further investigation suggested that the decrease in behavioral symptoms was most closely associated with an increased amount of parental supervision. Parents who moved out of poverty had more time to spend with their children. It was also likely that other factors, such as parental stress and depression, were also affected and had a positive impact on the children.

It is not poverty per se that causes delinquency, but rather the pervasive effect poverty has on the more immediate social and physical environment. Despite all this, most poor children are not antisocial;

however, poverty is a significant risk factor and increases the likelihood of problematic behavior in children along with other risk factors. Indeed, given the cumulative risk factors associated with poverty on the functioning of the child's family and their cognitive and physical development, poverty would seem to be the single most important factor associated with antisocial behavior in children. In particular, those children with biological predispositions associated with conduct disorder who are born into an impoverished environment would seem to stand very little chance of developing normally.

In 1997 approximately 20 percent of the population of individuals under the age of eighteen lived below the poverty level (Bureau of the Census, 1997). The rate for black and Hispanic youths was greater than one in three. Clearly this puts them at a great disadvantage right from the beginning of their lives.

Exposure to Violence

Most students of introductory psychology are taught about a famous experiment conducted in 1963 by psychologists Albert Bandura and R. H. Walters. In the study, a group of kindergarten children were shown a film of a little boy their age in a playroom behaving aggressively, hitting and kicking a large inflatable clown doll. Another group of children were shown a film with the same little boy, in the same setting, but showing him playing constructively with toys. One at a time, after observing the film, the children were put into the same playroom with the same toys, including the large inflatable doll, and their behavior was observed. Those children who saw the film of the little boy behaving aggressively were significantly more likely to behave aggressively than those who saw him playing constructively. In a second experiment, one group of children watched a film of a little boy behaving aggressively after which an adult came into the room and scolded him. The second group of children observed another film in which following the little boy's aggressive behavior an adult came into the room and praised him. When the children were placed into the same playroom, those who saw the little boy praised for aggressive behavior behaved aggressively themselves; significantly fewer of those who saw the little boy scolded behaved aggressively. From this, Bandura and Walters concluded that aggressive behavior is acquired through observation, although whether or not the child acts on that learning depends on what he or she perceives to be the consequences of that behavior. In other words, children are more likely to behave aggressively if they believe that their behavior will be rewarded.

Nancy Guerra and her colleagues followed a group of approximately forty-five hundred elementary school children aged five through twelve living in an inner-city Chicago neighborhood. They found that the children who were most aggressive reported greater exposure to violence, had more aggressive fantasies, and approved more of aggressive behavior (Guerra, Huesmann, and Spindler, 2003).

Children may also be routinely exposed to violence in the movies, television, and video and computer games. Studies have consistently demonstrated a relationship between violence on television and aggressive behavior. After a review of ten years of research, the National Institute of Mental Health (1982) concluded that violence on television leads to aggressive behavior in children and adolescents who watch those programs. More recent studies continue to confirm the association between media violence (including computer games) and aggression. Psychologist Craig Anderson and his colleagues note in an article reviewing research on media violence and aggression that even short-term exposure to violent media increases the probability of both physical and verbal aggressive behavior. Further, they note that longitudinal studies have found a relationship between exposure to media violence in childhood and aggressive behavior in adulthood (Anderson, Berkowitz, Donnerstein, Huesman, Johnson, Linz, Malmuth, and Wartella, 2003).

Protective Factors

Despite adverse environmental conditions, most children do not become conduct disordered or delinquent. This is often due to the presence of what are referred to as protective factors. These are factors, either within the child or his or her environment, which mitigate the danger or buffer the child against the negative effects of risk factors. It is only meaningful to think about protective factors to the extent that the child is exposed to significant risk factors. Just as with risk factors, protective factors may exist within the child or within the environment. Examples might include personal factors such as high self-esteem and a positive temperament or family factors such as good communication with parents and a positive nurturing relationship with at least one parent. An example of this might be a child with a mother who is particularly loving and supportive despite living under the stressful conditions associated with poverty and a neighborhood with a high crime rate. Protective factors in the environment could include relationships with supportive adults in the community such as a teacher or a minister. In addition, accumulating positive successful experiences for which the child or adolescent receives positive feedback—such as playing a musical instrument—can also serve as a protective factor. Psychologists Mary Carr and Trish Vandiver (2001) found that the presence of protective factors such as these reduced the likelihood of repeat offenses among a group of 76 adolescent first offenders.

Emily Werner conducted a longitudinal study of 698 children born in 1955 who lived on the island of Kauai in the Hawaiian archipelago (1987). About half of the children lived in chronic poverty and many of the mothers had less than eight years of formal education. Many had perinatal complications, developmental delays, and genetic abnormalities. In other words, these children were born with, and into, a high risk for developing behavior problems. In terms of protective factors that existed within the child, Werner found that being first born reduced the likelihood of later behavior problems, perhaps because first-born children are likely to receive more attention, at least early in life. Further, she found that children who were affectionate and responsive to people also had better outcomes, possibly because they generated more positive feedback from their social environment. In addition, children who were autonomous at an early age and had better communication skills also had better outcomes. Protective factors that existed within the child's environment included having fewer than five siblings (which means less stress on the family's financial and emotional resources), having had a lot of attention as an infant, having had a positive parent-child relationship during early childhood, and having had additional sources of emotional support available from other family members or neighbors—and later in life, teachers. Werner draws an interesting conclusion from her research: "The central component of effective coping with the multiplicity of inevitable life stresses appears to be a sense of *coherence*—a feeling of confidence that one's internal and external environment is predictable, that life has meaning and that things will work out as well as can be reasonably expected" (Werner, 1987, 42).

The psychologist Erik Erikson (1968) suggested that one of the foundations of adequate growth was the development of a sense of basic trust which is acquired during the first two years. It is the feeling that what exists outside oneself is available to meet one's needs and assist in maintaining an adequate physical and emotional balance. In this same vein Werner notes: "We were impressed by the pervasive effects of the quality of the mother-child interaction in infancy and early childhood that were documented as early as year one by home visitors and that were verified independently by the psychologists during the developmental examinations in the second year. They were also noted by the classroom teachers at age 10, and commented on by the youth in the age 18 interview" (Werner, 1987, 42).

Providing the child from infancy on, even under adverse personal and environmental conditions, with what he or she needs emotionally is apparently among the best protections against future behavioral problems.

Conclusions

In that children are born with different potentials and propensities and born into different environments, the needs of each child constitute a unique challenge. Unfortunately, many children who are born at greater risk for behavior problems receive insufficient protection from those risks, which only serves to amplify the likelihood of future difficulties. Much of the research on child development points to the importance of early childhood experiences in shaping future development. It is primarily the responsibility of the child's family to see that his or her unique set of needs are met. Individual factors such as drug abuse or mental illness, which interfere with the family's ability to attend to the changing emotional and physical needs of the child, increase the probability of future problems. In addition, the context in which the family lives can either create stress on child rearing or support it. Later in life, the ability of the educational system to meet the unique needs of the child is of great importance.

Children are born helpless and defenseless and remain that way for most of their childhood. It is the responsibility of families and society to see that their needs are met, for if they are not, the results can only create problems for the child and very possibly for society.

3

Adolescence and Delinquency

In his youth, everybody believes that the world began to exist only
when he was born, and that everything really exists for his sake.

Goethe

Daryl has an extensive delinquent history. At age thirteen he threatened another boy in his neighborhood with a knife and stole money
from him. The following year, with a group of other boys, he tried to
steal a bicycle from a grownup in the park, for which he was charged
with attempted grand larceny and attempted robbery. At fourteen, he
was arrested for car theft but the charges were dropped because of insufficient evidence. When he was fifteen he was arrested for selling
crack to an undercover police officer and, later the same year, his
mother filed a complaint saying that Daryl had hit her when she re-
fused to give him money. At sixteen he was charged with attempted
murder for shooting another teen who he believed was out to get him
for a drug deal that had gone bad.

Daryl's mother reported that she had had a difficult delivery with
him. He suffered from an oxygen deficiency (anoxia) at birth. He was
slow to begin talking and attended special education classes at school.
His academic skills were always poor, he had difficulty learning to read
and write, and he continued to suck his thumb into adolescence. He
behaved aggressively with other children at school and often had to be
separated from the rest of his class. Daryl's father was an alcoholic and
Daryl witnessed his father being physically abusive toward his mother

on a number of occasions. Daryl was found to have a number of minor neurological problems and was diagnosed as being mildly mentally retarded. If he were to live long enough and stay out of jail, according to current theory, it is likely that Daryl's antisocial behavior would decline as he got older. Daryl's behavior exemplifies the behavior of a seriously antisocial adolescent. His history is also typical. The antisocial behavior of childhood is exacerbated by adolescence.

In their book *Crime and Human Nature* Harvard professors J. Q. Wilson and R. J. Herrnstein note that "criminal behavior depends as much or more on age than on any other demographic factor—sex, social status, race, family configuration etc.—yet examined by criminologists. And it depends on age both in rate and type of offense" (Wilson and Herrnstein, 1985, 126). In fact, crime rates increase dramatically between the ages of ten and fifteen or sixteen, then level off and then decrease toward the end of adolescence and through the early twenties. The greatest rate of increase in antisocial behavior within the fewest number of years occurs during the early stages of adolescence, between the ages of twelve and fifteen. Figure 3.1 shows the arrest rate for violent crimes for the years 1980, 1994, and 2001. Note that while the arrest rates differ in each of these years the relationship between age and arrest rates is similar for all three years. This is not to say that children under the age of ten or eleven are not aggressive or assaultive, but it is much less likely that they will be arrested except in extreme instances, such as the case of the two ten-year-old boys in England who murdered a three year old. Furthermore, the terminology differs. Highly aggressive ten-year-old children are most likely to be labeled as conduct disordered whereas a highly aggressive fourteen year old is more likely to be identified as a juvenile offender.

Just as it is it not possible to understand behavior without considering the environmental context in which it occurs, it is impossible, I believe, to understand juvenile delinquency without understanding the unique developmental period of life in which it occurs. Despite the fact that delinquency is by definition an adolescent phenomenon, researchers in the field spend little time discussing the relationship between the two.

In the first comprehensive textbook on adolescence, written in 1905, the psychologist G. Stanley Hall referred to adolescence as a pe-

Arrests per 100,000 population

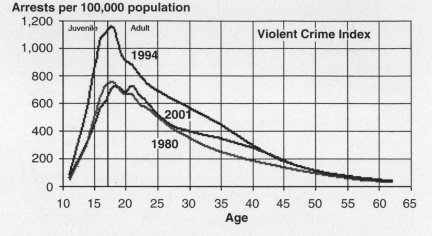

Figure 3.1. Violent Crime Index: Age-Specific Arrest Rate Trends. *Source:* Office of Juvenile Justice and Delinquency Prevention: www.ojjdp.ncjrs.org; accessed May 31, 2003.

riod of "storm and stress." Psychoanalysts agreed. They believed that adolescence was the inevitable result of the child's struggle to integrate the biological changes associated with puberty and sexuality into their existing personalities. Anna Freud (Sigmund Freud's daughter) went so far as to say (1958) that children who *did not* show signs of turmoil were the ones who were cause for concern. The concept of *identity crisis* reflected the psychologist Erik Erikson's belief that the inner struggle to define oneself was the central psychosocial crisis of adolescence, and created yet another reason for adolescent turmoil. Indeed Erikson suggested that a failure to find a positive identity in adolescence led some youngsters to seek out a negative one, in the form of delinquent behavior—a concept he referred to as *negative identity* (Erikson, 1957, 1968).

Not everyone agreed with Hall or the psychoanalysts. The anthropologist Margaret Mead suggested the stresses associated with adolescence were the result of cultural forces, not the inevitable outcome of biological changes associated with puberty. She spent several years in the 1920s observing adolescent development on the South Pacific island of Samoa. The results of her study were published in a book entitled *Coming of Age in Samoa* (1950), in which she described the lives of teenagers who did not have a particularly stressful adolescence. She believed that this was due to the fact that sexuality was more open and accepted in Samoan society and hence adolescents experienced less conflict around their own sexuality. Furthermore she noted young people's roles in society were more clearly defined by Samoan culture. She concluded that stress in adolescence was determined by culture not biology and therefore that adolescent "storm and stress" was not a universal phenomenon. Though the veracity of Mead's study has been challenged, it made a significant contribution to the continuing nature-versus-nurture debate. Most studies of adolescence, even those that find that most young people do not experience adolescence as a tumultuous period of life, find that some degree of stress, particularly in the early stages of adolescence, seems to be part of the process. It is often a time of increased conflict with parents, greater mood disruptions, and increased risk behavior (Arnett, 1999). It seems reasonable to wonder whether both the biological and social transitions associated with adolescence contribute to delinquent behavior. In other words, is the developmental process of adolescence itself a risk factor for antisocial behavior? It would seem to be, since by definition juvenile delinquency begins during the early stages of adolescence and starts its decline during late adolescence.

Risk Factors Associated with the Biological Transitions of Adolescence

Peter Blos (1962), a well-known child analyst who wrote extensively about adolescent development from a psychoanalytic point of view, suggested that adolescence could be better understood by dividing it into four periods or stages. He identified these as *preadolescence,* between ten and twelve years of age, *early adolescence* between twelve and fifteen years of age, *mid-adolescence* between fifteen and seventeen years of age, and *late adolescence* between seventeen to nineteen years of age. Breaking the adolescent years into stages takes into account the fact that the kinds of issues that a thirteen year old is responding to are significantly different from the issues faced by a seventeen year old. For instance, a thirteen year old may be dealing with the physical changes associated with puberty, whereas a seventeen year old might be struggling with the issues of having to earn a living or deciding what college to attend. Both are adolescents, but they are in considerably different places from the point of view of development and maturity and social expectations.

By the age of twelve or so, the approximate onset of adolescence, children already have experienced positive or problematical childhoods or something in between, so that stresses associated with adolescence are imposed on an already existing, though not completely formed, personality. Under normal circumstances, prior to adolescence, children will learn to follow rules, control their impulses, and acquire academic skills and knowledge. Typically these skills and behaviors are acquired both in school and at home, with each setting reinforcing the other. Children whose early years were marked by difficulties at home and/or at school, who failed to learn academically or socially, who were diagnosed with ADHD, conduct disorder, or other behavioral problems begin adolescence at a distinct disadvantage. And because they are less well prepared academically, socially, and emotionally to cope, their preexisting problems are often exacerbated by the biological and social stresses associated with adolescence. Note for example that Daryl, the boy discussed above, always had difficulty in school, as have a large majority of chronic delinquents.

From a biological point of view the most dramatic changes occur during early adolescence. Puberty usually begins around eleven or twelve for girls and somewhat later for boys. Puberty is associated with dramatic increases in hormonal levels for both sexes. Testosterone levels in boys may increase up to twenty times from their prepuberty levels between the ages of ten to seventeen; the greatest rate of hormonal increase occurs between the ages of twelve to fourteen in boys. There is an abundant amount of research on the effects of hormones and behavior in adolescence. While the findings are inconsistent, one truth that emerges is that the hormones affect different children in different ways and that girls are affected differently from boys (Buchanan, Eccles, and Becker, 1992). One recent study found higher levels of testosterone in fifteen-to-seventeen-year-old violent offenders when compared to nonviolent offenders of the same age (Brooks, 1996). Yet it would be wrong to conclude that testosterone, even though it has consistently been associated with aggressiveness in animals as well as humans, is the only factor responsible for the aggressive behavior in these youngsters. Not all violent offenders have high levels of testosterone, and most males with high levels are not violent offenders; most express their aggressiveness in socially accepted ways. However, for some teenagers high testosterone levels may intensify preexisting tendencies toward aggressive behavior. Also, it may not just be the absolute hormonal levels that create difficulties but rather the dramatic rate of increase that may serve to destabilize children who were not very emotionally stable or mature to begin with.

Neurological studies indicate that the brains of young adolescents are not fully matured, particularly the frontal lobes, which are associated with planning, judgment, and insight into behavior, all factors which would be associated with inhibiting impulsive behavior, or behavior that is driven by habit or biological forces. Thus the younger adolescent may be at risk because he or she is being energized and/or destabilized by increases in hormonal levels and at the same time does not have sufficient neurological maturity to contain those internal biological drives or resist external social forces. (Interestingly, this is a view that fits with the psychoanalytic conception of adolescent development which suggests that adolescence is the psychological adjustment to biological changes, although proponents of this theory rely less on empirical studies of biological development.) A neurological basis for antisocial behavior during adolescence gains further support from studies with known delinquents. These studies have fairly consistently found deficits in frontal lobe functioning in these adolescents, some of which have resulted from head injury or perinatal damage (Gorstein, 1990; Teichner and Golden, 2000).

Thus biological forces, along with social pressures, can serve to increase the likelihood of antisocial behavior in early through late adolescence. It is interesting to note that as the biological (and social) transformations of adolescence come to an end in late adolescence, so does delinquent behavior for most young people.

Factors in the Environment

Another notable change and potential risk factor associated with adolescence is an alteration in family relationships. Becoming emotionally independent of one's family is one of the developmental expectations associated with adolescence. This results in adolescents spending less time with their parents and family. One recent study found that seventh and ninth graders spend about half as much time with their families as do fifth graders. This results in less parental input and monitoring of children's behavior and also increased peer influence. Peer influence plays a significant role in determining adolescent antisocial and prosocial behavior. One recently completed study examined the behavior of approximately 3900 students from the eighth through the twelfth grade. The researcher found that the best predictor of misbehavior between the eighth and the tenth grade was negative (antisocial) peer influence, while the best predictor of misbehavior between the tenth and the twelfth grade was misbehavior in the tenth grade. However, if tenth-grade misbehavior was not included in the analysis, then antisocial peer pressure was the best predictor for the tenth through the twelfth grade as well. Interestingly, the best protective factor against misbehavior was positive peer pressure (Giancola, 2000). In other words, all through adolescence antisocial peer pressure is correlated with antisocial behavior.

Adolescents more frequently engage in antisocial behavior with their peers than do adults. In 1997, about 60 percent of robberies and 50 percent of aggravated assaults and other types of serious violence were committed by two or more adolescents acting together. An example is Robert, a sixteen-year-old boy whose parents brought him to see me because he had not been doing well in school and had been cutting classes. Psychological testing indicated that while he had no specific learning disabilities, he was of low normal intelligence. He told me that he never liked school very much, which is quite typical of teens that get into trouble. Robert began to hang out with other boys who weren't doing well in school. These boys were influential in Robert's life and gave him a sense of belonging to a group. They convinced him to take part in a series of burglaries which involved going into the athletic lockers of students while they were at a team practice, and stealing money from their wallets. They were eventually caught and Robert was put on probation. He told me that while he knew it was the wrong thing to do, it was hard for him to be the only member of the group who wouldn't participate in this illegal activity.

Delbert Elliot, who has written extensively in the area of delinquency, has proposed that for most adolescents it is exposure to delinquent peers that leads to delinquent behavior, as opposed to the other way around (Elliot and Menard, 1996). This suggests that to some degree adolescents learn to be delinquent from other adolescents. This is consistent with social learning theory described in the previous chapter, which proposed that aggressive behavior is acquired through observing aggressive models. It would also imply that adolescents living in high-crime neighborhoods would be more likely to engage in antisocial behavior, because they are exposed to more delinquent peers.

Related to this problem are concerns about juvenile gangs, more formalized groups of adolescents which may include young adults as well. Gang members are more heavily involved in delinquency than are nongang members. Furthermore gangs are responsible for a disproportionate amount of antisocial behavior. Research suggests that they facilitate preexisting antisocial tendencies in their members (Thornberry, 1998). Teens join gangs for a number of related reasons, including a need to belong, as a defense against isolation, as a search for a sense of identity, and as protection from other adolescents in the neighborhood, but the gang may also serve as an outlet and support for their antisocial tendencies in terms of increased social status from other gang members. Both boys and girls may be gang members, although boys outnumber girls by about nine to one. Most teens become gang members at around the age of fourteen, but in some neighborhoods they may express interest in joining a gang as young as nine years old.

Reliance on peers for antisocial behavior is consistent with adolescent development. The increasing physical and emotional detachment from the primary family leaves young people feeling increasingly "adrift," more dependent on peers for emotional and social support, and thus considerably more vulnerable to negative peer influences. Not all adolescents are at equal risk. Those with more problematic family relationships during childhood and during adolescence are more likely to feel alienated from their families, and thus more likely to identify with the antisocial values of their peers. Just as the quality of attachment to parents seems associated with behavior problems in childhood, it also appears to be true in adolescence. A study conducted by Dr. Joseph Allen and his colleagues at the University of Virginia found that adolescents who were anxiously preoccupied with their relationships with their mothers showed greater increases in delinquent behavior (Allen, Marsh, McFarland, McElhaney, Land, Jodl, and Peck, 2002). The need for security continues through adolescence, and even as adolescents strive for increasing autonomy from their parents, they need to have a safe emotional base to return to.

School

For most adolescents, the majority of time spent out of the home is spent in school. Schools serve as the primary source of social interaction for adolescents. While children in primary school are likely to return home at the end of the school day, adolescents are more likely to remain in the school for after-school activities or in the neighborhood of the school grounds. The transition from elementary to middle or junior high school and high school can also create problems both socially and academically. Primary school education ends around the beginning of adolescence, and junior high school (or middle school) represents a significantly different educational and social environment. The security afforded by a single classroom headed by a single teacher no longer exists, and the young person has the task of dealing with several teachers, each presenting a different set of challenges. A number of researchers have found that there can be a dramatic decrease in school performance associated with entry into junior high school. One study found that 45 percent of the boys and girls with good school records in primary school performed at only a poor level in junior high school (Finger and Silverman, 1996). The effects are even more pronounced in large urban schools, where records of students indicate that the most significant decreases in academic performance occur in the first year of the transition to middle or high school (National Research Council, 1993). More importantly, children who have experienced academic and behavioral problems in the early grades are going to find the higher levels of education more difficult and frustrating, increasing the likelihood of truancy or dropping out completely. In addition, adolescents who fail to relate academically and socially are more likely to be marginalized by their peers. These teenagers are more likely to find themselves relating to other adolescents having similar difficulties, who in turn are more likely to engage in truancy and other forms of antisocial behavior. They are also more likely to be suspended or expelled from school, further increasing their isolation.

Schools may not always be safe places. Thirty-seven percent of high school students surveyed reported that they had been in a physical fight. Interestingly, it was the younger students who more often reported fighting. Forty-five percent of the ninth graders said they had been involved in a fight, compared to only 29 percent of the twelfth graders. Four percent of these adolescents required treatment by a doctor or a nurse. The period of time immediately after school is apparently not so safe either. Serious violent crime—including aggravated assault, assault with a firearm, and sexual assault—peaks at the hours just as school lets out, suggesting that many juvenile crimes are committed within the vicinity of the school grounds. As a result, 4 percent of high school students reported missing a day of school in the past thirty days because they felt unsafe either at school or traveling to and from school. It was the younger adolescents who were more frightened. Twice as many ninth graders (6 percent) reported avoiding school as did the twelfth graders (3 percent) (Office of Juvenile Justice and Delinquency Prevention, 1999).

Weapon use, particularly guns, is a problem. A 1997 survey found that 9 percent of high school students said that they had taken a weapon of some type, including a knife, gun, or club, to school during the past thirty days. Many of the adolescents who carried weapons said they carry them for protection from other students, a concern which may have some merit since 7 percent of all high school students reported being threatened with a weapon sometime during the school year. The National Institute of Justice found that 20 percent of juveniles who are arrested carried a gun all or most of the time (National Institute of Justice, 1997).

Also of concern are the recent episodes of school shootings in Arkansas and Colorado in which students, in seemingly senseless acts of violence, shot and killed their fellow students and teachers. There was no apparent motive for the shootings; they were not fights over girls, or with particular teachers, or revenge killings for personal grudges. In response to the shootings, the Federal Bureau of Investigation convened a panel of psychologists, psychiatrists, and other professionals to determine the underlying causes for these events (Federal Bureau of Investigation, 2000). It is important to note that these types of mass shootings at school, while horribly tragic, are relatively low probability events. None of the students involved in these shootings had significant histories of delinquency that would have suggested that they would engage in such destructive behavior, although it is always possible from hindsight to identify potential problems. A more obvious case is the recent school shooting on an Indian reservation in Minnesota. A sixteen-year-old youth killed his grandparents and then went to his high school, where he shot and killed a number of students and teachers and a security guard, after which he shot and killed himself. The young man had a history of psychiatric problems. He described himself as a loner and seemed preoccupied with violence. He wrote about being physically abused by his alcoholic mother. Unfortunately, his difficulties were not noted by the school administration.

The FBI panel did note risk factors which can exist in the individual student, his family, the school setting, and in society which can contribute to this behavior. Risk factors in the individual's personality included low tolerance for frustration, poor coping skills, depression, alienation, excessive need for attention, and lack of trust in others. Family factors that were noted were turbulent parent-child relations, parental acceptance of pathological behavior, lack of intimacy, and access to weapons. School dynamics that might create problems included the student's lack of attachment to school, the school's tolerance for disrespectful behavior, inequitable discipline, and the social dynamics of the school culture. Also noted as potential problems were access to violent media, peer groups, substance abuse, and the copycat effect. The panel concluded that in most instances no one factor was decisive, or, on the other hand, without potential effect. They did not address the more commonplace day-to-day violence that exists in the schools as noted above, which while less dramatic is considerably more problematic for the typical student.

I have tried to make the point that adolescence, particularly early adolescence with its associated biological and social transitions and stresses, puts youngsters at a higher risk for antisocial behavior than perhaps any other stage of life. These stresses and transitions exacer-

Table 3.1. Childhood versus Adolescent Onset of Behavior Problems

Behavior during childhood	Behavior during adolescence
(1) no behavior problems	no behavior problems
(2) conduct disorder	no behavior problems
(3) conduct disorder	conduct disorder/delinquency
(4) no behavior problems	conduct disorder/delinquency

bate difficulties in children with already existing conduct disorders, making them more antisocial and violent. It is these children who are more likely to go on to have adult criminal careers. Adolescence also creates antisocial behavior in a very large number of children who had no apparent histories of conduct disorder prior to adolescence.

With regard to the onset of conduct disorder/delinquency there are four possible combinations of childhood/adolescent behavior (see table 3.1).

Psychologist T. E. Moffit (1993) suggested that juvenile delinquents could be divided into two types, childhood onset and adolescent onset. Childhood onset is associated with high-risk personal characteristics, such as subtle cognitive deficits, difficult temperament, hyperactivity, and a high-risk social environment, which might include inadequate parenting, disrupted family bonds, poverty, and poor relationships with peers and teachers. This type of background more typically results in antisocial behavior that continues into midlife.

The second and more common type of delinquent is that which she refers to as adolescent onset. Adolescent onset begins at around the time of puberty. These adolescents more typically engage in less violent behavior and their criminal activity usually ends during late adolescence (approximately eighteen years of age).

A recent study by psychologist Michael Windle (2000) illustrates this point. Windle took measurements of self-reported antisocial behavior every six months from 975 adolescents (half boys and half girls) between the ages of fifteen and a half to seventeen and a half years of age. Antisocial activities ranged from relatively minor transgressions such as skipping school to more serious offenses such as stealing and assault. One of his findings was that about 5 percent of the participants in the study were persistent offenders. That is, they engaged in relatively high levels of antisocial behavior during the two years of the study. Furthermore, they engaged in a wide range of delinquent behavior ranging from relatively minor offenses to criminal behavior. Eleven percent of Windle's sample reported not engaging in any delinquent behavior, and 84 percent said they engaged in some delinquent behavior but not as much or consistently as the persistent offenders. For most adolescent offenders the rate of delinquent behavior initially increased, reaching a peak at around mid-adolescence (about sixteen years of age) and then decreased after that. One of the important differences between the persistent offenders and those whose delinquent behavior was limited to their adolescent years was that the persistent offenders reported more childhood conduct disorders and more alcohol and marijuana use. The chronic offenders also reported a more rapid rate of increase in terms of the number of offenses they committed from age fifteen through seventeen. As a group, the persistent delinquents reported less family support, more friends who used alcohol, a more difficult temperament in childhood, and lower school grades than the offenders whose incidents were restricted to the adolescent years.

Windle's findings are consistent with the results of other studies on delinquent behavior. First of all, the percentage of chronic delinquents, approximately 5 percent, is consistent with other studies such as the Philadelphia cohort study by Wolfgang reported above. (He found about 6 percent were persistent offenders.) This backs up the findings that while the large majority of adolescents engage in some degree of delinquent behavior (about 84 percent in this study), a small percentage is responsible for a large amount of the delinquent behavior. Secondly, it suggests that for most adolescents, delinquency is limited to the teen years. In Windle's study, delinquency increased, for most adolescents up until sixteen or so, and then decreased.

What makes this interesting with regard to adolescence is that both the increase and decrease in antisocial behavior are linked with increases and decreases in the levels of developmental stress associated with adolescence. As adolescents begin to accommodate to the biological and psychosocial transitions associated with adolescence, usually around the middle to later stages of adolescence, there is also a decrease in the amount of antisocial behavior. However, there is also that small percentage of teenagers for whom the antisocial behavior during adolescence is a continuation of behavior problems which began in childhood. For these youth the stresses associated with adolescence may exacerbate an already problematic personality structure. August Aichhorn (1935), a Viennese analytically inclined educator, suggested that some children develop what he referred to as a latent delinquent character structure. These are basically children who, because of reasons of temperament or life circumstances, fail to develop adequate controls over their impulses and thus are more prone to delinquent behavior during adolescence. One of Windle's findings was that the more persistent delinquents had more difficult temperaments, for example, they tended to be more oppositional and hyperactive as children, and that a more rapid decline in delinquent behavior toward the end of adolescence was associated with a less difficult temperament. Another important difference between the persistent offender and the adolescents whose antisocial behavior was limited to their teen years is that the latter group tended to engage in less serious offenses.

It is not just age that is associated with antisocial behavior; it is what is going on developmentally for the individual at that time of his or her life. Just as neglect or abuse can increase the likelihood of antisocial behavior because of the developmental problems it creates in terms of feeling attached to others, so can being adolescent increase the likelihood of delinquency because the biological and psychosocial stresses make the control of antisocial behavior more difficult. Arrest rates rise more rapidly during early adolescence for two reasons. One is that children younger than ten are rarely arrested and rarely have the physical or cognitive wherewithal to commit serious offenses. The second is that early adolescents are under the greatest amount of developmental stress both biologically and socially.

It seems clear that as parents and as a society we are not providing enough of our adolescents with the crucial support and structure that they need during this difficult time of life. A recent survey of adolescents from fourteen to seventeen years old, reported in the *New York Times* by an organization called Fight Crime, found that 38 percent of teenagers were not supervised after school for three or more days a week (Rothstein, 2002, B8). Those who were unsupervised were twice as likely as supervised teenagers to drink, five times as likely to take drugs, and four times as likely to commit crimes or misdemeanors. While it is unlikely that it is the lack of supervision alone that generates this behavior, the absence of structure is likely to be a contributing factor.

Substance Abuse, Mental Illness, and Conduct Disorder

Psychiatric disorders often present in clusters of two or more. For example, depression and anxiety often coexist. This is referred to as comorbidity. The origins of mental illness and substance abuse, like the origins of conduct disorder and delinquency, are multiple. They lie within the individual's biological makeup and his or her immediate environment and history. For example males with alcoholic fathers are more likely to become alcoholics than males with nonalcoholic fathers. (This is true even if they have no contact with their fathers.) Because children with conduct disorder typically grow up under adverse conditions, they often suffer not only from conduct disorder but from other psychiatric disorders as well. The most commonly diagnosed co-morbid disorder occurring with conduct disorder in children is attention deficit hyperactivity disorder (ADHD) (Kazdin, 1996).

ADHD has two components. The first, attention deficit, refers to the inability to stay focused on and follow through with a task, as well as the tendency to be easily distracted by extraneous stimulation. The second, hyperactivity-impulsivity refers to the inability to control motor impulses. Children who are hyperactive often are constantly fidgeting, getting out of their seats, blurting out answers, or interrupting or intruding on others. The two aspects, attention deficit and hyperactivity, may appear separately or together (see table 3.2).

In a large-scale study of the relationship between mental health problems and antisocial behavior in youth, the psychologist Rolf Loeber and his colleagues noted that ADHD and conduct disorder were the two psychiatric disorders that were most closely associated with delinquency and that children with ADHD often show signs of conduct disorder earlier in life and are more aggressive (Loeber, Farrington, Stouthamer-Loeber, and Van Kammen, 1998). ADHD often ap-

Table 3.2. Diagnostic Criteria for Attention Deficit/ Hyperactivity Disorder

This diagnosis requires *six* or more instances of inattention or hyperactivity over a six-month period of time. It also requires that some of the symptoms have been present prior to the age of seven and that the symptoms create significant problems in school and/or social settings.

Inattention

1. fails to give close attention to details or makes careless mistakes in schoolwork or other activities
2. difficulty in attending to tasks or play
3. doesn't seem to listen when spoken to
4. doesn't complete work or chores at school or home
5. has problems organizing tasks
6. avoids tasks or activities that require sustained attention
7. loses things necessary for school or other tasks (e.g., books)
8. easily distracted by irrelevant stimuli
9. often forgetful

Hyperactivity/impulsivity

1. fidgets or squirms
2. runs or climbs around when inappropriate
3. doesn't remain in seat when appropriate (e.g., in a classroom)
4. difficulty in engaging in quiet leisure-time activities
5. seems to be in perpetual motion
6. talks excessively
7. blurts out answers
8. doesn't wait for his/her turn
9. interrupts or intrudes on others

Source: Adapted from American Psychiatric Association, *Diagnostic and Statistical Manual of Mental Disorders* (2000), 83–84.

pears in children whose parents have had ADHD. It also is associated with child abuse or neglect, the use of drugs by the mother during pregnancy, and multiple foster home placements. The histories of children and adolescents with ADHD are very similar to those with conduct disorder/delinquency. Clearly such children would have difficulty learning in school, where being able to focus and demonstrating self-control are expected and necessary for learning, and could be very problematic at home as well. Because of their behavior, children with

ADHD are much more likely to do poorly in school and receive negative feedback from teachers and parents, leading to lower self-esteem
and a greater propensity to behave badly. Not all children with ADHD
have conduct disorder, nor do all children with conduct disorder have
ADHD, but the combination of the two seems to be very problematic
and sets young children off on a very dangerous trajectory.

Substance abuse is another commonly occurring problem among
delinquents. Loeber and his colleagues, in the same large-scale study
on mental illness and antisocial behavior, found a direct relationship
between substance abuse and delinquency, as have numerous other
studies. These researchers found that among eighth graders with serious delinquent behavior problems, 36 percent reported using hard
liquor, compared to 22 percent who were only minor offenders; in addition, over 80 percent of the serious offenders reported using marijuana or other illegal substances, compared to only 1.4 percent of the
minor offenders.

There are two issues of importance relating to substance abuse.
One is that some substances, such as alcohol, reduce inhibitions, and
as such may serve as a catalyst for antisocial acts. There are numerous
studies that connect alcohol with violent behavior. Thus the combination of alcohol in adolescents already prone to antisocial behavior is
quite dangerous. Other substances, particularly stimulants such as co-
caine, crack/cocaine, and amphetamines, also increase the likelihood
of antisocial behavior. Adolescents who abuse illegal substances often
need money to pay for them and this money frequently is obtained
through antisocial behaviors such as burglary, robbery, or drug dealing. It is not difficult to understand that substance abuse can result in,
and usually is intimately related to, delinquent behavior.

The causes of serious substance abuse are similar in part to the
causes of antisocial behavior: a history of substance abuse in the family,
neglect, school failure, high propensity for risk taking, social isolation,
and depression. Adolescents often abuse drugs as a way of masking and
coping with other psychological problems such as depression and anxiety. Depression and anxiety often occur along with conduct disorder.
One study found that between 15 to 31 percent of children referred for
conduct disorder also received the diagnosis of depressive disorder
(Zoccolillo, 1992). The rates of anxiety disorder among children who

are seen in clinics for conduct disorders has been reported to be as high as 75 percent.

Anxiety disorders and depressive disorders are referred to as internalizing disorders, because when either or both of them occur in the absence of conduct disorders, they typically do not result in antisocial behavior; instead the problems are focused inwardly. The fact that they are present in many instances of conduct disorder may indicate that there is a factor common to these disorders and conduct disorder, just as in substance abuse and ADHD.

Psychiatrist Michael McManus and his colleagues investigated a group of seventy-one incarcerated seriously delinquent adolescents (McManus, Alessi, Grapentine, and Brickman, 1984). There were forty males and thirty-one females in the study, all with backgrounds that were quite problematic. Fourteen percent had had a change in custody by the time they were ten years old, 72 percent had experienced the loss of a parent through death, divorce, or separation, 46 percent had suffered from physical abuse, neglect, or abandonment (this was even more true for the females, almost two-thirds of whom had dealt with some sort of abuse). There were indications of psychiatric illness in 31 percent of the parents of these teenagers, and 31 percent of the parents had been arrested at some point. Almost two out of three of the adolescents (63 percent) suffered from substance abuse and or alcoholism. Forty-four percent were diagnosed as having borderline personality disorder, and 38 percent had some form of mood disorder. In addition, schizophrenia or schizophrenic-like symptoms were observed in 39 percent of the delinquents. (Note: The numbers do not total to 100 percent because all of the adolescents received more than one diagnosis.)

I had the opportunity to meet with the court psychologists responsible for evaluating adolescents who were referred to the family court in New York City. All adolescents who are charged with violent crimes are required to have a psychological evaluation. The psychologists told me that the most common diagnosis of these adolescents was conduct disorder, and second, borderline personality disorder (BPD). This was consistent with McManus's study, which found that BPD occurred at a very high rate among incarcerated delinquents. Personality disorders differ from other diagnoses in that they are seen as more a pervasive characteristic of the individual's personality as opposed to a circumscribed set of symptoms, such as are found in anxiety or depressive disorders. According to the DSM IV, the diagnostic criteria for BPD include unstable interpersonal relationships, impulsivity, unstable mood, inappropriate intense anger, difficulty controlling anger, transient stress-related paranoid ideation, or severe dissociative symptoms (American Psychiatric Association, 1994). These personality characteristics frequently describe delinquents who typically are angry, impulsive, and given to attributing hostile intentions to others. While most people who are diagnosed with BPD are not delinquents or criminals, they do frequently share similar childhood histories of neglect and abuse, underscoring the point that early childhood adversity leads to damaged adolescents and adults, even when it doesn't result in delinquency.

Are chronically delinquent adolescents "mentally ill" or are they just "bad"? The answer depends on the perspective one takes. From a social point of view, from the perspective of their victims, they are "bad." They commit multiple offenses, their crimes are often violent, and they are frequently indifferent to the considerable pain and suffering they cause others. From a psychological perspective they frequently suffer from neurological and diagnosable psychiatric disorders. Conduct disorder is both a psychiatric disorder and at the same time a symptom of multiple underlying problems. An often quoted study by psychiatrist Dorothy Lewis and her colleagues compared thirty-one incarcerated delinquents to thirty-one nondelinquents (Lewis, Pincus, Lovely, Spitzer, and Moy, 1987). The delinquents showed greater evidence of psychopathology, including paranoia, auditory hallucinations, and suicide attempts. They manifested a significantly greater number of minor neurological problems. They were more likely to have been abused and have been witness to family violence. Their mothers were more likely to have had a psychiatric hospitalization, and they were more likely to have had an out-of-home placement. Seriously delinquent adolescents differ significantly from nondelinquent or minor delinquents in a number of important ways other than their antisocial behavior. To focus on just the antisocial behavior at the expense of the numerous other difficulties these adolescents typically have presents a distorted picture of who they are.

Female Delinquency

Sara, who is seventeen, was arrested and charged with aggravated arson and burglary. She had started a fire along with a friend in an apartment from which she had been recently evicted. She had been living in the apartment with a boyfriend. The owner of the building said that Sara and her boyfriend had probably been involved with using and selling drugs. Sara said she started the fire because she wanted to get even with people who had stolen from her and that she also wanted to damage the building.

Information gathered from Sara's mother indicated that Sara had always had difficulties in school. As early as kindergarten she had gotten reports from Sara's teachers that she talked out of turn and had trouble controlling herself. In her early teens she began to run away from home. The mother admitted that Sara's running away might have been the result of being abused by the mother's boyfriend.

Sara said that she uses hostility and anger to keep people away from her. She said that she was very angry about being sexually abused as a child. She also reported excessive use of drugs including alcohol, marijuana, and LSD and reported a history of minor offenses, but denied prostitution for drug money. The psychologist who examined Sara found that she was depressed, anxious, and potentially suicidal (although apparently she had no immediate intent to harm herself).

Sara's history is typical of female delinquents. She does not have a history of violent offenses. The crime for which she was arrested did not involve direct confrontation with the victim. She has a history of being abused and running away and comes from an unstable family. Her psychiatric symptoms of depression and anxiety also frequently occur in female delinquents. However, like serious male delinquents, she has a history of chronic behavior problems; as well as being a delinquent, she is also a victim.

Although females are less likely to become delinquent than are males, rates for female delinquency have been increasing rapidly over the past years without any apparent explanation. Most research on delinquency has been done with male offenders, at least in part, because there are so many more of them. Boys are arrested much more frequently for all offenses, with the exception of running away (probably to avoid sexual abuse) and prostitution.

For example, in 2001 females accounted for 28 percent of all arrests for individuals under the age of eighteen, about 18 percent for violent crime, and about 31 percent for property crime (Snyder, 2003). The important question to be addressed is whether, despite the differences in delinquency rates, the same risk factors that apply to boys also apply to girls, and whether or not there are other factors which are unique to female delinquents. If important differences between boys and girls do exist, then different interventions (prevention and treatment) would be required.

Certainly one of the more obvious reasons for the fact that more boys than girls are involved particularly in violent antisocial behavior is that they are acculturated differently. Boys play with toy guns; girls play with dolls. Aggressive behavior is more likely to be reinforced in boys than it is in girls. As they go through adolescence, boys are physically stronger and thus more capable of violence (although guns could serve as an equalizer). But also many of the risk factors associated with conduct disorder are more common in boys. These include more symptoms of nervous system dysfunction, difficult temperament, greater degree of learning disabilities, more attention deficit disorder, and a greater frequency of hyperactivity. Given this, boys are more likely, as a group, to generate negative feedback from caretakers and teachers early in their lives.

Terri Moffit (Moffit and Caspi, 2001), the same researcher who proposed differences between childhood-onset versus adolescent-onset delinquent behavior, looked at a group of about one thousand children from age three through age eighteen. She hypothesized that the risk factors for both males and females would be similar for both childhood-onset as well as adolescent-onset conduct disorders. What she found was that boys outnumbered girls in terms of the childhood-onset antisocial behavior by ten to one, but only by two to one in adolescent-onset antisocial behavior. In other words, boys are much more likely to display antisocial behavior earlier than girls, but girls are much more similar to boys in terms of displaying antisocial behavior during adolescence. What was also quite interesting was that both the childhood-onset boys and the childhood-onset girls had *similar* backgrounds.

Both boys and girls tended to come from families in which discipline was harsh and inconsistent and family conflict was high. Parents and teachers of both the boys and the girls reported them to be difficult and hyperactive and given to fighting. Both had difficulties with peer relations as well. In addition, both showed neurological difficulties at age three. While this suggests that both boys and girls with chronic behavior problems may share similar backgrounds, it doesn't explain why boys are considerably more likely to have such problems in the first place, or conversely, why girls are so much less likely to begin behaving this way.

One of the more likely explanations for the difference in rates of early conduct disorder for boys and girls may lie in the fact that boys are different both genetically and neurologically. Boys are much more likely to exhibit neurological problems early in life than girls. Boys are also more likely to exhibit problems including mental retardation, autism, stuttering, learning disabilities, attention deficit disorder, and hyperactivity (Lynman and Henry, 2001). Social and cultural factors also play a role, since aggressive behavior is more likely to be encouraged and tolerated in boys than it is in girls. So a combination of biological and environmental factors is likely to contribute to the significant differences among childhood-onset behavior problems. The differences are much less notable when comparing adolescent-onset behavior problems, which for the most part tend to involve less serious delinquent behavior. In her research, Moffit found that with the exception of peer relationships, the adolescent-limited delinquent boys' or girls' backgrounds did not differ significantly from their nondelinquent contemporaries.

Outcomes in Adulthood

In the previous chapters I have tried to summarize the research which consistently demonstrates that delinquent children and adolescents come from adverse family backgrounds, have failed in school and in their interpersonal relations, have come to see the world as a hostile and indifferent place and respond to it in kind. Approximately 30 to 40 percent of early-onset conduct-disordered adolescents go on to have criminal careers. Antisocial behavior is one of a number of possible outcomes for children who have grown up under adverse conditions and experienced the beginnings of their lives in this way. Those who do not become antisocial because of their temperament frequently suffer from depression, alcoholism, and other psychiatric disorders. They are more likely to be unemployed or homeless, have difficult marriages, fail as parents of their children, and have shorter life spans (Maugan and Rutter, 2001). For example, psychologists Katja Kokko and Lea Pulkkinen found that children who were rated as aggressive by their teachers at age eight were more likely to exhibit school maladjustment at age fourteen and then more likely to suffer from long-term unemployment in their adult years (Kokko and Pulkkinen, 2000). As I noted earlier, we cannot expect normal or reasonable behavior from children who are raised under abnormal or unreasonable circumstances, nor can we expect them to grow into a normal adult life any more than we can expect a plant to grow normally in the absence of adequate light and water.

Conclusion

Children are transformed by their experiences while growing up. How they are transformed and what the behavioral outcomes of those experiences are depends upon who they are at that moment in time, what their biological predispositions are, and what their prior experiences have been. Some children, regardless of how awful their lives have been, will not become antisocial; others will become delinquent with having had minimally adverse experiences.

Ultimately, it is the responsibility of our society to see that children get what they need as they develop. We are well aware of what the needs are. It is unreasonable to expect that children who are deprived of adequate housing and safe neighborhoods, who are abused, neglected, and poorly educated will grow up to be happy, productive citizens. I have shown in the previous two chapters how the failure to meet those needs can result in delinquent behavior. It is not unreasonable to see these children as victims as well as delinquents. While some might argue that this is a politically liberal position to take, it is not. Rather it is a reflection of the consistent findings over a large number of years of social science research. Children cannot choose how they are treated or where they live. They are very much at the mercy of their adult caretakers. Most children receive the love, attention, and education they need. Unfortunately some do not, and there is little they can do about this. They are sent into their adolescent years on a trajectory that dooms them to failure. Those with biological constitutions that predispose them to aggressive behavior become dangerous predators. But that is of our making. In the next chapters I will look at the ways in which we, as a nation, have responded to this problem.

4

Social Response
Rehabilitation and Retribution

When, in countries that are called civilized, we see age going to the workhouse and youth to the gallows, something must be wrong in the system of government.

Thomas Paine

At the age of fourteen, Marco was arrested and held in jail after he was accused of sexually molesting his seven-year-old sister. He admitted to the charge and apologized to his family. Even though he had no prior offenses, he was nonetheless charged as an adult. In Arizona the law mandates a minimum of five years in prison for sex offenders. He was placed in the only adult prison in Arizona that accepts juveniles, a facility that has no treatment program for juvenile sex offenders. The psychologist who evaluated him said that he was in need of treatment and that he did not believe that Marco represented a significant risk in terms of victimizing other children. After spending a year in the county jail, Marco said that he now knew how to start fights and that "when the new guys come, they look at me like I'm supposed to tell them what to do, like I'm the old timer" (Talbot, 2000, 96).

In 1997 9,100 adolescents under the age of eighteen were being held in adult jails. While most of them were held for person-related offenses, about a third were held for property, drug, and public-order related offenses. A disproportionate number of them were minorities (U.S. Department of Justice, 1999, 208).

Had Marco been arrested in another state the response might have been considerably different. He might have been referred to a treatment program or placed on probation. Society's response to juvenile offenders is frequently inconsistent and illogical and often not based on the needs of the child. Two youths with pneumonia, one in Alabama and the other in New York, would likely receive the same medical treatment. However, two youths who committed the same offense, with similar backgrounds, risk factors, and personalities are likely to receive very different types of responses depending on four variables: the state and jurisdiction in which the offense was committed; the types of programs that are available; the laws affecting juvenile offenders; and the decisions made at intake by the court workers and family court judges.

An attorney for the juvenile division of the Legal Aid Society in New York responsible for defending adolescents in family court told me that one of the major problems he found in representing youngsters was the level of inconsistency that exists within the family court system. A study conducted by the community defenders clinic at the New York University School of Law (2001) found that youths brought before the family court in one borough might be twice as likely to be incarcerated, as opposed to being released on parole, as in another borough. The study also found that the decision to remand (detain in a jail) as opposed to parole was not based on the seriousness of the crime but rather on other incidental factors, such as the presence of a family member in court at the time of the hearing and/or reports of family or school problems.

I have already pointed out that about 6 percent of all teenagers engage in seriously delinquent behavior and are responsible for more than 60 percent of all of the crime committed by adolescents. If we knew that 6 percent of all adolescents would suffer from some type of physical disorder or from some serious form of psychiatric disorder, we would make a concerted effort to either prevent this disorder from occurring in the first place or find a cure for it once it had occurred. Yet the prevalence of conduct disorder and delinquency over the past fifty years has not changed appreciably. The research conducted by Wolfgang, which I described in chapter 1, found that the later-born cohorts of children were becoming more violent.

In 2001 the surgeon general of the United States, Dr. David Satcher, issued a report on youth violence which noted that in 1999 there were 104,000 arrests of youths for violent crimes, including robbery, rape, aggravated assault, and homicide. The primary emphasis of the report was to define youth violence as a public health issue, with an emphasis on prevention as opposed to rehabilitation. Dr. Satcher asked the Centers for Disease Control, the National Institute of Health, and the Substance Abuse and Mental Health Administration—three agencies within the Department of Health and Human Resources—to contribute to the report. It is important to note that none of these agencies is part of the criminal justice system. This fact reinforces the schism that exists within society. One view is that delinquency is criminal behavior in individuals under the age of eighteen who, under certain circumstances, can be tried in adult criminal courts and incarcerated. The other view considers delinquency as a symptom of a childhood and adolescent psychopathology which is in need of mental health services. The conflicts that led to the establishment of the juvenile court over one hundred years ago have never been resolved.

On its most basic level, a public health approach deals with disease through prevention and treatment. Prevention requires knowledge of factors which are associated with the causes of a particular disease. We know that the incidence of lung cancer is higher among the population of people who smoke. Prevention programs are defined in different ways and directed at different segments of the population. Primary prevention programs are designed to prevent the occurrence of a disease. A campaign directed toward school-age children to prevent them from beginning to smoke in the first place is a good example of primary prevention. The same would be true in the case of delinquency. Primary prevention would entail identifying and modifying risk factors and early precursors to delinquent behavior. Primary prevention programs for delinquency lie outside of the criminal justice system.

Treatment, however, deals with a disorder, physical or mental, once it has already been established in the individual. In the field of delinquency these may be referred to as treatment programs, borrowing from the public health model, or sometimes as rehabilitation programs, a term used in the criminal justice system. In this chapter the focus will be on treatment programs for adolescents who either show early signs of antisocial behavior or conduct disorder in childhood, and for those who have broken the law and come into contact at some level with the criminal justice system. The lines between what constitutes prevention and treatment often can get blurred, since treating a ten year old with conduct disorder may also be designed to prevent later law-breaking antisocial behavior. Such treatments are sometimes referred to as secondary prevention interventions, since they are designed to prevent further escalation of a problem that already exists. However, secondary prevention interventions, such as family therapy, may be described as a prevention strategy in one source and as a treatment approach in another.

The Legal Response

Society responds to adolescents who break the law through either the juvenile court or through the adult criminal justice system. The intent of the juvenile court is rehabilitation, not punishment. Adolescents appearing before the juvenile court are often referred to rehabilitation or treatment programs. On the other hand, the intent of the adult criminal justice system is more punitive than rehabilitative. Adolescents who are convicted after appearing in adult courts may receive no help with their problems.

A juvenile's first contact with the juvenile justice system is typically a street encounter with the police. The police have a fair amount of discretion in terms of how they will handle a particular incident, depending upon the nature of the offense, the status of the victim, the attitude of the juvenile (varying from contrite to hostile), the directives given to the police by the community (which can range from tolerance to a get-tough policy), etc. Police may have contact with the juvenile either through a direct stop on the street or as a result of a complaint from a victim. Most police-juvenile encounters are for nonviolent crimes such as public disorder, status offenses, and petty theft. In most instances, the police will deal with the street encounter informally by warning the juvenile regarding the potential consequences of further contacts. Actual arrests occur in approximately 15 to 20 percent of the cases. Juveniles are much more likely to be arrested if the offense is serious, if there is compelling evidence, if a victim is present, if a weapon is found, or if the adolescent's attitude toward the arresting officer is hostile. Even when taking the offender into custody, the police may deal with the matter informally. About 25 percent of juveniles taken into custody are released with a warning and a notation in the station records.

The remaining cases are submitted to juvenile court. (See table 4.1 for a breakdown of the basic process of the juvenile justice system.) When a juvenile is referred to the court, the case first goes through an intake process in order to determine whether to proceed to a formal adjudication hearing. The intake process is generally conducted by an intake officer and/or the prosecutor's office. About half of the cases referred to intake are not referred for further processing but are dealt with informally, or "diverted" from formal processing in the juvenile court. In these instances, the youth may acknowledge the charges and agree to certain conditions such as attending school, making restitution to the victim, or attending a treatment program of some type. While this initial investigation might be an opportunity for a careful investigation of the needs of the child, it frequently is not. Margaret Rosenheim, who served as a consultant to the President's Commission on Law Enforcement and the Administration of Justice, points out that cases are rarely screened carefully, because intake workers have more cases than they can reasonably handle. Therefore the emphasis is on making quick, rather than thoughtful and deliberate, decisions (Rosenheim, 2002).

Juvenile courts were first established in Illinois in 1899 and later adopted by other states. The purpose of the court was twofold. One was to divert the adolescent away from the adult criminal justice system. The second, based on the assumption that the adolescent's antisocial behavior reflected problems that he was having in his life, was to intervene in the life of the adolescent so that these problems could be addressed. The function of the court was to rehabilitate, not punish. Juvenile courts also differ from adult courts in that the adolescent is not tried before a jury, and until 1967 was not represented by an attorney. Since the purpose of the juvenile court was to help the child, not punish him, neither a jury nor a defense attorney was necessary. Beginning in the mid-1960s, certain procedural changes were made to pro-

Table 4.1. Juvenile Justice System: Basic Process

The overarching purpose of juvenile justice is to rehabilitate young offenders. The key components of the system are the juvenile court, the state juvenile justice agency, detention, corrections, and probation. Children coming into contact with the system in different states will have their cases processed in very different ways. But there are some decision points that are common to every case. The following describes what might happen to one child, Michael, who comes into contact with the system.

Initial contact
Like around 85 percent of kids in the system, Michael comes into contact with juvenile justice by referral from law enforcement.

Intake: Formal or informal processing
After Michael is referred, "intake" (probation or the prosecutor's office) decides whether to handle his case informally or formally.

Informal case processing: Dismissal or voluntary treatment
Around half the cases are "informally processed"—either dismissed or handled out of court. If Michael's case is not dismissed, probation or the prosecutor will ask him to agree to take certain actions, such as restitution or counseling, for a set period of time. If Michael complies with this voluntary agreement, his case will be dismissed. If he violates the agreement, he may be referred back to the court—and this time his case will be processed formally.

Formal case processing: Adjudication—or trial as an adult
Formal case processing starts with an intake petition for either an adjudicatory hearing or a waiver hearing—which could result in Michael's transfer to adult criminal court. In thirty-six states, state law requires that certain cases be automatically handled in adult criminal court, although twenty-three of those states allow the criminal court judge to waive the case back to juvenile court. In fifteen states, prosecutors have discretion to file a waiver petition to the adult criminal court for handling the youth's case.

Pre-adjudication: Detention or release
After his arrest, Michael may be held in detention until his case is processed. Within twenty-four hours the court must hold a detention hearing to determine whether he should be detained or released until the next hearing.

Adjudicatory Hearing: Guilty or innocent
If intake has petitioned for an adjudicatory hearing, the juvenile court holds the hearing to determine whether Michael committed the offense.

(continued)

Table 4.1. (*Continued*)

Waiver Hearing: Trial as a juvenile or an adult

If intake has requested a waiver hearing, the court convenes to determine whether Michael's case should be waived to adult criminal court.

Disposition: How to handle the case

If the court determines that Michael committed the offense and adjudicates him "delinquent," juvenile probation prepares a "disposition plan" that recommends how his case should be handled, e.g., with treatment, counseling, probation, or secure corrections. The juvenile court then holds a "disposition hearing" where the judge decides on the final disposition plan.

Review hearings: Is the disposition plan working?

Throughout the term of the sentence the juvenile court holds review hearings to determine whether Michael is complying with the terms of his probation, or to determine the length of his confinement.

Aftercare: Rehabilitation and parole

After release from secure corrections, Michael may be placed in aftercare, or "juvenile parole," under the supervision of the juvenile court or the juvenile justice agency.

Source: Office of Juvenile Justice and Delinquency Prevention, retrieved December 29, 2003, from www.ojjdp.ncjrs.org.

tect juveniles' rights to due process, including the right to have a defense attorney present.

This right was based on a United States Supreme Court decision made in 1967 known as In re Gault (387 U.S. 1, 1967). Gerald Gault was a fifteen-year-old Arizona boy who made an obscene phone call to his neighbor. (He asked her on the phone whether she had "big bombers.") He was brought before a juvenile court judge without being notified of the charges against him and he was not represented by an attorney. His neighbor did not appear in court; the testimony against him was provided by the arresting officer, who read the neighbor's account of what had happened. Gerald Gault was committed to an Arizona state training school for six years. Had he been an adult and found guilty of the same charge, his punishment would have been considerably different. He could have received a fine of not more than fifty dollars or been sentenced to not more than two months in jail.

Gault challenged his adjudication as a delinquent all the way to the U.S. Supreme Court. The court found in his favor, saying that his status as a juvenile did not deprive him of his Fourteenth Amendment rights to due process. This meant that even in juvenile court, youngsters had the right to counsel, a notice of the charges against them, and the right to confront the witnesses against them.

Dramatic increases in the juvenile crime rate in the late 1980s through the mid-1990s led states to change the laws regarding juvenile delinquents, making it easier to transfer juveniles to adult courts, allow for expanded sentencing options, and change the confidential nature of juvenile court hearings. All states now allow, or mandate, that juveniles be transferred to adult criminal courts depending on the nature of the offense, the juvenile's prior history of offenses, or the juvenile's age. Marco, the fourteen-year-old boy who molested his sister, is an example. There are a number of mechanisms for transferring adolescents accused of crimes to adult criminal court. One is on the basis of age, although the absolute age varies from one state to another. In New York, Connecticut, and North Carolina the juvenile courts have jurisdiction for adolescents up to fifteen years of age; youths aged sixteen and older are tried in adult criminal court regardless of the nature of the offense. Other states have maximum ages of up to seventeen years of age.

There are a number of other legal and administrative mechanisms for transferring adolescents to adult court. Some states make transfer to adult courts automatic, based on the nature of the offense and/or the number of prior adjudications for felonies. This is known as statutory exclusion. Practically every state provides the juvenile court judge with the discretion to send an adolescent to adult criminal court. This judicial discretion is presumably based on a balance of the needs of the adolescent, and his amenability to rehabilitation, versus public safety needs. However, there are laws in many states that limit the discretionary power of the juvenile court judge, in effect mandating waiver to adult court (National Research Council, Institute of Medicine, 2001). In some states, depending on the offense, the prosecutor rather than the judge has the discretion whether to send the case to juvenile or adult court.

While one might imagine that it is only the more serious offenses that are sent to adult court, this is not always the case. More than half the adolescents sent to adult court in Florida between 1979 and 1981 had committed serious property offenses; only 29 percent were waived to criminal court for person offenses, i.e., crimes such as robbery, rape, and assault. The percentage of youths sent to adult courts and the type of offense they have committed also varies from one state to another. There are no national guidelines.

Sentencing has also become more punitive. As noted above, over nine thousand youths under the age of eighteen are being held in adult jails, although, according to federal guidelines, they must be segregated from the adult population. Sentencing guidelines now include mandatory minimum sentences and blended sentences, which follow detention in juvenile facilities with transfer to an adult facility when the adolescent reaches a certain age.

The Supreme Court in a five-to-four split (*Roper v. Simmons*, 2005) recently ruled against imposing the death penalty for individuals who committed capital crimes when they were less than nineteen years old. Citing research studies, Justice Anthony Kennedy, writing for the majority, noted that juveniles differed from adults in a number of important ways, including a lack of maturity, greater susceptibility to negative influences, and more transitory personality traits, and as such were less culpable. Up until the decision, capital punishment for individuals who were minors when they committed their crime was an option in twenty-three states (Greenhouse, 2004). Over the past thirty years 225 individuals received the death sentence for crimes they committed as minors (under the age of eighteen). Of these, twenty-two were executed, most of them in Texas. Seventy-three remain on death row. The remainder had their sentences reversed or commuted. The United States was one of the few countries that allowed for the execution of individuals under the age of eighteen. The Court recently ruled against the practice of executing those who were mentally retarded when they commit such offenses.

While in practice relatively few juveniles are tried in adult court, and relatively few receive extensive sentences, the existence of laws allowing for trying juveniles as adults and punitive rather than rehabilitative sentencing reflects a marked change in society's response to delinquency. As with many other policy decisions, this harsher response has not proven to be effective. Juveniles transferred to adult courts are more likely to continue offending than are those who remained in the juvenile court. Furthermore, juveniles who are incarcerated are more likely to re-offend when released than those placed on probation.

A recent study conducted by criminologist Jeffrey Fagan (1995) compared fifteen and sixteen year olds charged with robbery or burglary. One group was tried in adult court, the other in juvenile court. Those tried in adult court for robbery were significantly more likely to be found guilty and incarcerated than those tried in juvenile court. (These differences did not exist for those tried for burglary.) Adolescents tried in adult court did not receive longer sentences than those whose cases were tried in juvenile court. However, Fagan found that those tried in adult court were more likely to be rearrested and reincarcerated than those who were tried in juvenile court. Adolescents tried by adult courts were also more likely to be rearrested within a shorter period of time. On the basis of this study it appears that neither of the presumptive reasons for trying adolescents in adult courts—retribution and public safety—is accomplished. Juveniles do not receive longer sentences in adult courts, hence their punishment is not worse, and they are more likely to re-offend, so the safety of the public is not enhanced. Criminal justice researchers Barry Krisberg and James Howell conclude: "In sum, there is remarkably little evidence that transferring juveniles to the criminal justice system produces any positive benefits" (Krisberg and Howell, 1998, 356).

Other factors that need to be taken into account when adolescents are tried in an adult criminal court are the issues of competency to stand trial and culpability or criminal responsibility. Competency refers to the adolescent's ability to understand the charges brought against him, to understand the nature of the legal proceeding, and to participate in his own defense. Culpability refers to the *degree* that an individual who is found guilty of an offense should be held responsible for it. For example, someone who was suffering from a serious mental illness at the time of a crime might been seen as less responsible or culpable than someone who was fully aware of what he or she was doing and what the consequences of the behavior could be.

The MacArthur Foundation (2004) has established a research network on adolescent development and juvenile justice. Among the outcomes of this project have been a study on adolescents' competence to stand trial and a book entitled *Youth on Trial* (2000), edited by psychologist Thomas Grisso and attorney Robert Schwartz. The study defined "serious impairment" as insufficient knowledge, understanding, and reasoning to a degree that would indicate that the individual was incompetent to stand trial. The researchers found that adolescents between the ages of eleven and thirteen were three times more likely to be seriously impaired than young adults aged eighteen to twenty-four and that adolescents between the ages of fourteen and fifteen were on average twice as likely to fall into the category of seriously impaired as young adults. Furthermore, those adolescents who had below average intelligence (IQs of less than 85), which is more common among the juvenile offender population, are even more likely to be seriously impaired.

Another recent study found that younger age, lower intelligence, and higher suggestibility affected adolescents' ability to understand their Miranda rights (Redlich, Silverman, and Steiner, 2003). For example, 44 percent of the juveniles thought that "waiting for the police to ask you a question meant the same as having the right to remain silent" (403). The study also found a strong relationship between the ability to understand Miranda rights and competency to stand trial.

With regard to culpability, psychologist Lawrence Steinberg and attorney Elizabeth Scott (2003) question whether juveniles should be punished in the same way as adults who have committed comparable crimes. They suggest that from a developmental point of view adolescents are less able to make rational decisions than are adults. They cite research studies that find that adolescents are more susceptible to peer influence, more likely to discount risk and long-term consequences, and less able to control emotional impulses. Steinberg and Scott believe that these differences between adults and adolescents result in what they refer to as "diminished culpability," which should lead to a judicial policy of mitigated punishment. While they were specifically concerned with the application of the death penalty to adolescents convicted of capital offenses, these assumptions could be applied to other categories of offenses as well. Their opinions were important in determining the Supreme Court ruling against the execution of seventeen and eighteen year olds.

Apparently, not only is it ineffective to transfer juveniles to adult court, in many instances it may not be very fair either. Juveniles are transferred to adult courts on the basis of public perception and legislative response, not on the basis of what is known and what is effective. It is as if the Food and Drug Administration approved a procedure that wasn't effective, based on public perception rather than on the basis of scientific evidence.

Pre-adjudication Detention

A juvenile may be detained in a secure facility at any point from the time he is arrested until after a formal family court hearing. The reasons for detention may be based on concerns that the adolescent represents a threat to the community, will fail to appear for a hearing, is in need of psychological or medical evaluation, would benefit from residential treatment, or needs to be "taught a lesson." Despite research conducted in this area, the ultimate reasons for detaining a youth prior to a hearing remain unclear (McCord, Spatz-Windom, and Crowell, 2001). In a report issued on detention by the Correctional Association of New York, a former youth officer from the New York City Police Department was quoted as saying, "Sometimes spending a night in jail is all it takes for a young person to learn his lesson. . . . Even if we are not supposed to put kids in jail for that reason it does happen" (Faruquee, 2002). State laws require that a detention hearing be held within twenty-four to forty-eight hours. At the hearing a decision is made to either release the youth or continue the detention. About one in five adolescents is held in detention prior to a formal hearing.

About 38 percent of juveniles detained are held for property offenses, 26 percent for person-related offenses; the remainder are held for public-order offenses, drug law violations, and status offenses. Minorities are disproportionately represented among youth held in detention. For 1996 black adolescents accounted for 30 percent of the delinquents processed and 45 percent of youths detained (Office of Juvenile Justice and Delinquency Prevention, 1999). In New York City, more than 95 percent of detained adolescents were black or Latino (Faruquee, 2002). As noted above, because so much discretion is allowed, a fifteen year old could be detained for up to two days for possession of a small quantity of marijuana, if his attitude at the time he was stopped was hostile toward the arresting officer.

The average length of stay in detention centers has increased from approximately twenty to thirty-six days, largely because of over-burdened court systems (Faruquee, 2002). The effects of detention can be quite traumatic for adolescents because it separates them from their family, friends, and school. Conditions in detention centers vary. Some provide adequate mental health and educational services and others do not. The majority of children are detained in facilities that are overcrowded, leading to an increased likelihood of altercations with staff and other juveniles. A juvenile being held for minor offenses may be detained in the same facility as youths being held for more serious offenses, increasing the probability of negative peer pressure and/or victimization.

Yet, alternatives to pre-adjudication exist. New York City established an Expanded Alternatives to Detention program for youths making their first appearance before the family court. While the program is successful in retaining adolescents in the program and guaranteeing their appearance in court, it fails to provide the children with adequate educational facilities during the time they are assigned to it. Since many of the adolescents are seriously deficient in academic skills, this represents a major shortcoming. Alternatives to detention programs have been established in other parts of the country as well, including Broward County in Florida, Cook County in Illinois, and counties in the state of Washington. These programs have developed techniques for evaluating risk and reducing racial disparity within the system. The early evaluations of these programs suggest that they can be successful. Approximately 90 percent of the youths appear for their scheduled hearing and do not re-offend during this period of time. These are much more in the spirit of the juvenile court acts which emphasize the least restrictive alternatives (Faruquee, 2002).

Secure Placements

Once adjudicated, the equivalent of being found guilty in criminal court, adolescents may be placed in a residential or community setting away from home, or placed on probation. There are competing interests here, however. Placing a youth in a secure facility offers the community greater protection from further offending, at least for the period of time he is placed. But, in keeping with the intention of the juvenile court, the placement should be in the best interest of the child and should provide adequate educational and mental health services. However, this is not always the case. A report in the *New York Times* (March 1, 2005) noted that the care received by juveniles in detention facilities may be quite inadequate. The article describes the cases of two teenage girls suffering from major depression and bipolar disorder, who were incorrectly taken off their medication and prescribed medication for ADHD instead. As a result, both girls' conditions deteriorated (von Zielbauer, 2005).

Ideally, there should be nationwide uniformity in the way placement decisions are made; facilities ought to meet certain standards of service, as well as physical standards. There should be evidence that a large majority of youths leaving the facility perform better than when they entered, the standards that one would expect from any good residential mental health facility. Unfortunately this is not the reality. There is a large variation from state to state in juvenile correction policies. Some facilities are operated by local governments, others at a county or state level, and some are operated by private agencies. According to a report by the Office of Juvenile Justice and Delinquency Prevention, facilities are generally overcrowded and violence and escapes are not uncommon (Parent, Leiter, Kennedy, Livens, Wentworth, and Wilcox, 1994).

There is an ongoing debate over whether or not confinement halts or accelerates criminal behavior. Often this is a policy debate between those who want to get "tough on crime" versus those who take a more liberal position, but it is a debate which is rarely informed by empirical data. The evidence is equivocal. There is some data that support the idea that youths who have been incarcerated are slower to re-offend and, certainly from a public safety point of view, there is benefit in removing a habitual offender from the streets. An additional problem associated with detention is the racial discrepancies. In 1997 the overall juvenile male custody rate was 620 per 100,000. For white males it was 327 per 100,000 but for black youth the rate was 1,776 per 100,000—more than five times the rate for whites. The custody rate for Hispanic adolescents was 902 per 100,000, almost three times the rates for whites. Clearly minorities are disproportionately represented in juvenile detention facilities, a problem which has not yet been adequately addressed.

Overall however, it is doubtful that significant progress has been made in terms of the judicial and legal responses to antisocial behavior in adolescents. Consider the remarks made in 1926 by William Healy and Augusta Bonner, a psychiatrist and a psychologist, in their book *Delinquents and Criminals*: "It is amazing that modern civilization, with all its frank devotion to the conceptions of efficiency, has not yet undertaken thoroughly critical studies of what are the results of its dealing with delinquency and crime. Despite the tremendous equipment and expenditures for protection, detection, apprehending, for courts, jails and prisons, reformatory education, probation, little or nothing is spent to ascertain with care what is or is not accomplished. In industry, business or active science, such an inquiry into results is regarded as absolutely fundamental" (Healy and Bronner, 1926, 3). They continue: "It is the experience of our selves and many other observers that different judges and other officials have entirely different and opposed scales of values according to which they decide upon treatment. There is no compendium from which to teach, for example, whether your shoplifters, or forgers, or sex offenders, of certain types and having had certain experiences, tend or not to reform under constructive probation or other treatment" (Healy and Bronner, 1926, p. 9). Unfortunately, the situation has not changed a great deal in three quarters of a century: "The unplanful almost chaotic procedure of the present in dealing with delinquency and crime is perfectly obvious to any student of the subject. Very frequently and at any stage what is done has a strange irrelevance to anything that has been done before or in many cases what is likely to be the outcome" (Healy and Bronner, 1926, p. 225).

Some eighty years later the researchers Barry Krisberg and James Howell state in a review of sanctions for juvenile offenders that "we know little more today about the efficacy of targeted enforcement and suppression programs than we did two decades ago" (Krisberg and Howell, 1998, 353). They continue by stating that the question of whether "traditional juvenile correctional interventions or adult style punishments exert positive, neutral, or negative impacts on youthful criminal careers has not yet been answered" (364) and then go on to say, "Given the enormous fiscal and human consequences of various sanctioning approaches, it is tragic that our research base is so slender. In particular, juvenile corrections policies and practices, and the movement to transfer more youths to adult prisons, are informed by anecdotes, flawed research and media popularized fads. Juvenile and criminal justice policies freely and quickly moved from 'scared straight' to 'tough love,' from boot camps to chain gangs" (364).

That a conclusion such as this can be drawn more than a hundred years after the establishment of the juvenile court and more than seventy years after Healy and Bonner's comments is extremely troublesome. A good example of the fact that these problems continue to exist is the study I mentioned earlier in this chapter which found that whether a juvenile was remanded or released on probation was more a function of the borough in which the offense occurred than the background of the delinquent or the nature of the offense.

The Treatment Response

At any point during the juvenile justice process the adolescent may be referred to a treatment program, either to attend one based in the community or to be placed in a residential facility. The effectiveness of these treatment programs can vary greatly. The concept of nonmedical interventions for certain types of psychological disorders originated with Sigmund Freud toward the end of the nineteenth century. Freud believed that some of the physical symptoms that patients experienced had a psychological basis, and he developed the technique of psychoanalysis to uncover the causes of these psychological disorders. Subsequently this technique was applied to a much wider range of disorders, including anxiety and depression. Freud posited that problems or conflicts in early childhood led to problems in later life, and that reasons for an individual's feelings and behaviors were often hidden from them in their "subconscious." While Freud has been subjected to considerable criticism over the past hundred years, many of the basic tenets of his theory of behavior remain. For example, much of the research on juvenile delinquency supports Freud's idea that early childhood experiences are critically important to understanding behavior later in life.

Freud had little experience treating children or with theorizing about, or working with, individuals who exhibited antisocial behavior. However, the fundamental concepts of psychoanalytic theory were applied to the understanding and treatment of delinquents as early as 1917 by William Healy, who was affiliated with the court clinic in Chicago. He said the following: "I would like to emphasize the most fundamental of all facts concerning this subject, namely, that the use of the genetic [relating to the history of the child] method opens the way, as nothing else does, to the most formidable attacks upon misconduct. One might expect any toughly common-sense method to include an effort to go back to the beginnings in order to arrive at understandings, yes, and in order to accomplish reformations, although this only too seldom accords with actual practice" (Healy, 1917, 15).

Healy was followed in Austria by August Aichhorn. Aichhorn, whose work with juvenile delinquents was based on psychoanalytically informed education, wrote: "Every child is at first an asocial being in that he demands direct primitive instinctual satisfaction without regard for the world around him. This behavior, normal for the young child, is considered asocial or dissocial in the adult. The task of upbringing is to lead the child from this asocial to a social state" (Aichhorn, 1935, 4).

One other major publication from psychoanalytically oriented practitioners on treatment of delinquents was entitled *Searchlights on Delinquency* (Eisler, 1949). It was an edited book, published in 1949, and contained a number of interesting chapters on the causes and treatments of antisocial behavior from a psychoanalytic point of view. The psychoanalysts had little to say about delinquency after that, although there were occasional publications. Their work is rarely referred to in the literature today, despite the fact that many of their ideas, including the emphasis on early childhood experiences and the importance of the family environment, are integrated into the current thinking about the causes and treatment of delinquency.

A second major impetus for treating delinquents came from behaviorism. This school of American psychology, founded by John Watson in the early twentieth century, believed that all behavior, normal and abnormal, was learned, and that the proper subject of psychology was the study of observable behavior. It was antithetical to psychoanalysis, which was focused on unconscious conflicts. The behaviorists believed that Freud's psychoanalytic theory was "unscientific." B. F. Skinner, in the middle of the last century, was a strong proponent of behaviorism. He proposed that all behavior was determined by its consequences. Positive consequences reinforce behavior and thus increase the likelihood of its repetition. Negative consequences reduce the likelihood of a behavior occurring again. These not so complicated notions were applied to the origin and treatment of a wide range of problematic behaviors. According to the behaviorists, antisocial behavior was learned according to the same principles as pro-social behavior. Following from this assumption, treatment focused on reinforcing desired behaviors and ignoring or punishing antisocial behavior. This conception differed from that of the analysts, who felt that antisocial and aggressive behavior was an inherent part of human nature and that the child, with the help of family and school, had to learn to control it.

There were also a group of psychologists who took a middle-ground position. These were the social learning theorists and the cognitive psychologists. They believed that mental processes, although not necessarily unconscious ones, played a central role in affecting behavior. They suggested that it was not only the external situation (or stimulus) that determined the response but also how the individual processed it. Treatment for delinquents derived from this theoretical perspective focused on providing better role models and correcting distorted ways of thinking about situations, such as learning not to perceive all intentions of others as hostile.

There were also proponents who saw delinquent behavior arising in a social or family context, and made use of what is called systems theory. The focus of this approach to treatment is understanding and working with the individual within the context of his psychosocial environment. Problems don't just exist within the individual adolescent; they also exist within the family context in which he or she is living. Both the environment and the individual may be problematical and in need of modification. Various family therapies are based on this assumption.

In taking a pragmatic and eclectic approach to therapy, treatment might occur in the school, at home, or in the neighborhood. Treatment could be configured in any number of ways, including family, group, or individual therapy. In those instances in which the adolescent or her family is felt to be too problematic for her to remain at home, treatment is conducted within the confines of a foster home, an institution, in some instances a prison. Whatever the modality, and there are quite a number of them, ranging from "boot camps" to religious indoctrination, their primary goal is, or should be, to improve the lives of these youngsters and to reduce or eliminate antisocial behavior. How successful they are at reaching this goal is another matter.

Some Basic Tenets of Treatment

When adults seek treatment they generally do so voluntarily. They accept the fact that they have a problem and believe that talking to someone about it will be helpful to them. One of the key factors in determining the outcome of therapy has to do with receptivity. Critical factors are willingness to work on the problem, an acceptance of personal responsibility for the problem, and a belief that the therapy will be helpful.

A second important factor in the therapy is the relationship that is formed between the patient and the therapist. Therapy needs to be carried out in the context of a relationship in which the patient trusts the therapist, believes that the therapist understands him or her, and believes that the therapist is competent enough to be helpful. For example, a recent study evaluating multisystemic therapy (see below), a treatment for seriously delinquent adolescents, found that its success was dependent on the quality of the relationships the therapists were able to establish with the families they were working with (Huey, Henggeler, Brondino, and Pickrel, 2000).

Given that these conditions are met, therapy is often helpful. Interestingly, the specific theoretical orientation of the therapist usually does not play a major role except in instances of specific problems, such as phobias, where seeing a behavioral therapist might be best indicated. Most therapists define themselves as eclectic, so they are likely to apply a wide range of techniques.

However, when we consider the treatment of delinquents, the situation is quite different. First of all, few delinquents enter treatment voluntarily. Most often they are required to do so either by their families or by the courts. Secondly, they are more than likely not to believe that they have a problem. Adolescents in general tend to blame others—teachers, parents, and police—for their difficulties. Finally, they are not likely to believe that talking to anyone about anything is going to do them much good. Given that motivation, personal responsibility, and a belief in therapy are some of the most important variables affecting the outcome of therapy, these delinquents are not off to a good start.

The other important variable, the relationship that is formed between the therapist and the client, is also problematic for adolescents. Most delinquents have had difficulty with relationships all their lives. They are not likely to enter into such an arrangement with a great sense of trust. On the contrary, mistrust is more likely to be the watchword.

Another difficulty associated with the development of treatment programs is establishing which problems will be addressed. Ostensibly, any program will have as its goal a significant reduction in antisocial behavior. Serious delinquents typically have multiple problems that underlie and presumably form the basis for their antisocial behavior in the first place. They often have serious academic difficulties; many are seriously behind their grade levels in basics such as reading and mathematics. They are likely to have problems with drugs and/or alcohol; many, as I have pointed out, may suffer from psychiatric disorders including depression, anxiety disorders, ADHD, substance abuse, and personality disorders. They may come from, and ultimately be returned to, environments which are likely to be psychologically toxic, such as abusive or neglectful families and/or neighborhoods with poor housing and high crime rates. If these adolescents are going to be helped, all of these issues would need to be addressed. This is a monumental task.

Typically, treatment programs are created based on what the programs' developers believe are the primary underlying causes of the antisocial behavior. If they believe inappropriate family interactions are at the root of the behavior, then a primary goal of the program would be to improve family interactions. This might be accomplished through parent training programs and/or family therapy sessions. Programs might also focus on inappropriate attributions, academic skills, anger management, developing empathy, etc. Many programs attempt to address a number of different problems simultaneously. However, in all instances, there needs to be a relationship between what issues are addressed or treated and what the program administrator believes to be the underlying cause(s) of the antisocial behavior. Other factors that need to be taken into account include whether the treatment would take place while the adolescent resides in the community, or whether he is placed in a residential setting such as a group home or a state training school.

Treatment Programs

Unlike in medicine, there are no agreed upon treatment protocols for modifying the behavior of all delinquents. Delinquents are a heterogeneous group of individuals, so that it is unrealistic to assume that any one approach would be appropriate for all of them. Secondly, as noted, delinquent behavior is very often the tip of the iceberg since these teenagers frequently have academic and psychiatric problems that need to be addressed as well. In order to be effective, a treatment intervention should be tailored to the specific problem or problems the individual has, for example substance abuse and depression. It is often very difficult to address the multiple problems that exist within the adolescent's psychosocial environment, which may include family unemployment, drug abuse, poor housing, and high levels of crime in the neighborhood.

Interventions for delinquent behavior can range from release with a warning to complex programs that deal with various aspects of the adolescent's environment. Before discussing specific approaches, it would be helpful to understand how these programs are evaluated, since in describing them I will also discuss outcome results.

Fundamentally, an evaluation is an experiment. In most instances, there will be an experimental group, or the group that receives the treatment, and a control group that receives no special treatment. The characteristics of the group receiving the particular treatment and the control group must be similar. Often this is accomplished by randomly assigning adolescents to either the treatment group being evaluated or to a routine probation program (or some other form of control group). The two groups would have to be similar in terms of average age, number of prior offenses, seriousness of the offenses, etc.

Prior to the implementation of the study, a decision is made regarding what measures will be used to evaluate the effectiveness of the program. A long-range goal might be reduced recidivism as measured by contacts with the police or self-report. A program might also have intermediate goals as well, such as improved academic or social skills. It is important that these goals be defined in such a way that they can be measured objectively, for example by teachers' rating scales of the teenagers' behavior or tests of their reading levels. After a specified period of treatment, perhaps six months to a year, the agreed upon measurements would be taken from both the treatment and control groups and follow-up measurements of antisocial behavior might be obtained up to a year or more after the adolescents were discharged from the program. The results of the measurements of the two groups could then be statistically compared in order to determine whether the treatment group showed significantly more improvement on the specified goals than the control group. Since any given program might not have very many participants, the data from a number of similar programs are frequently statistically combined into what is known as a meta-analysis, which, because it analyzes a much greater number of program participants, provides greater statistical confidence in the outcomes.

Other questions that are addressed in a program evaluation include whether or not the program was carried out as described in the proposal and whether the program was more effective for one type of delinquent than another. Program evaluations are designed not only to determine the effectiveness of a program but also to determine what aspects of the program are effective and with what types of individuals. They ought to provide feedback that allows not only for the verification of an approach, but that allow for that approach to be modified and improved upon.

In 1998, psychologists Mark Lipsey and David Wilson published a review article of over two hundred programs designed to treat both institutionalized and noninstitutionalized serious juvenile offenders. All of the studies included in the review made use of a control group; half of the youths received the treatment interventions provided by the program, whereas the other half might have simply met with a probation officer or been sent to an institution that did not provide treatment. Most of the adolescents included in the studies were white males (approximately 40 percent) between the ages of fourteen and seventeen. Just about all the youths were adjudicated delinquents. Most had a mixed background of offenses, including person and property crimes, and two-thirds had a history of aggressive behavior. Lipsey and Wilson performed a statistical analysis combining the compared difference between the treatment and control groups of all two hundred programs (a meta-analysis).

This analysis found that, overall, 50 percent of the youths who did not receive treatment continued to commit offenses, whereas only 44 percent of those who received treatment continued to offend. (This outcome was very similar to the findings of a similar meta-analysis on 126 institutionalized adolescents completed about fifteen years earlier [Garrett, 1985]. The consistency lends credence to the results, although it also suggests that perhaps the situation hasn't improved much with time.) The difference was statistically significant, meaning that it was very unlikely that the differences between the groups was due to chance. On the other hand, it is not a very large difference either.

The analysis also found that some types of interventions were considerably more effective than others. For example, programs that focused on individual counseling, improving interpersonal skills, and using behavioral techniques were much more effective in reducing recidivism than were wilderness programs and probation and parole programs. For programs designed to work with institutionalized delinquents, interventions which focused on improving interpersonal skills and used a group home with counselors, employing behavioral techniques, were also more effective than wilderness challenge, drug abstinence, and employment related programs. I have reproduced a summary of their findings in table 4.2.

Another notable finding was that key characteristics, including the number and type of prior offenses, a history of aggressiveness, and the age and ethnicity of the adolescents, were important in determining outcome. The more serious offenders seemed to get greater benefit from the programs, although it isn't clear why this was the case. For institutionalized adolescents, the results indicated that programs that had been established for a longer period of time were more effective than newer programs and that treatments administered by mental health professionals were more effective than treatment administered

Table 4.2. Summary of Effectiveness of Treatment Intervention

Noninstitutionalized delinquents:	Institutionalized delinquents:
Strongest evidence for positive effects	
Individual counseling	Interpersonal skills
Interpersonal skills	Teaching-family home
Behavioral programs	
Less consistent evidence but generally positive effects	
Multiple services	Behavioral programs
Restitution, probation/parole	Community residential
	Multiple services
Mixed results	
Employment related	Individual counseling
Academic programs	Guided group
Advocacy/casework	Group counseling
Family counseling	
Group counseling	
Weak or no demonstrated effectiveness	
Reduced probation/parole caseload	Employment related
Wilderness	Drug abstinence
Early release	Wilderness
Deterrence programs	Milieu therapy
Vocational programs	

Source: Adapted from M.W. Lipsey, and D. B. Wilson (1998), Effective intervention for serious juvenile offenders: A synthesis of research, in R. Loeber and D. P. Farrington (eds.), *Serious and violent juvenile offenders* (Thousand Oaks, CA: Sage), 313–345.

by juvenile justice personnel. This might have been the case because the juvenile justice personnel were perceived by the adolescents to be authorities, and thus less understanding. Other factors that affected outcome for both institutionalized and noninstitutionalized delinquents were the amount of treatment the youths received (more is better) and the type of treatment they received. As noted, some treatment approaches were clearly found to be better than others.

What is lacking in this analysis is what kind of intervention is best for what kind of adolescent. One of my first jobs after graduate school was evaluating a delinquency treatment program. The program was designed to be an alternative to institutional treatment. The twenty-five boys in the program attended the school-based program during the day and went home in the late afternoon after the end of planned after-school activities. During the day, in addition to attending small classes (generally five boys per class) there were also large and small group meetings where boys could discuss personal or interpersonal problems, groups for the parents, and the availability of individual counseling. Each boy was also assigned to a "special teacher" who would help him with a variety of problems, including getting medical attention, helping out with court appearances, dealing with administrative problems within the school, etc. This teacher also served as a role model for the boy. After working there for a while, I devised a small study in which I asked each of the five teachers whether, based on their experience of at least three months or more with the boy, they felt the program was the right place for him to be (Brandt, 1979). Of the twenty-five boys included in the study, the teachers felt that the program was suitable for only half of them. The boys who had a long history of behavior problems based on their prior school records, and whose testing suggested that they had a greater degree of psychopathology, were seen as less suitable. (The teachers were unaware of the school histories or the test results when they answered the question about the boys' suitability for the program.) The problem didn't lie so much with the design of the program as with its attempt to address too wide a range of problems. Retrospectively, it was a good place for adolescents who were not so seriously delinquent, even though it was designed to work as an alternative to institutionalization. The lesson is that because of their wide range of underlying problems, not all antisocial adolescents can benefit from the same types of treatment intervention. Unfortunately, it is not always possible to match up the adolescent with the program. Some need more structure than others; some need more psychiatric support, others more academic support. Only large programs that are able to provide a wide range of quality services can serve a wide range of delinquents.

It is also worth noting that some interventions can have negative effects. Researchers Thomas Dishion, Joan McCord, and Francois Poulin (1999) point out that an estimated 29 percent of treatment programs result in an *increase* in antisocial behavior. They reviewed the data from several studies to test the hypothesis that negative outcomes result from grouping antisocial peers together within the same setting.

They found that in the programs they reviewed conduct-disordered adolescents were likely to support and reinforce, and sometimes encourage, the deviant behavior of their peers. This resulted in worse rather than better behavior. This was the case in the program I described above. A number of boys who had not been substance abusers began to use them as a result of being influenced by boys in the program. Dishion and his colleagues suggested that this might be avoided through mixing treatment groups with more boys who had already made positive changes in programs and were more prosocial. I had the opportunity to visit a residential program for delinquent youth in Quebec, Canada. After spending a brief period of time in a reception cottage, the boys in this program were placed in cottages with participants who had been in the program for a longer time and thus had made progress toward reaching behavior goals. The program made successful use of positive peer influence.

Specific Approaches to the Treatment of Delinquents

Discussing specific approaches to treating antisocial behavior is complicated by the fact that therapies may take place in three different settings: while the adolescent is living at home, in a group or foster home where the adolescent has been removed from his or her own home but still may attend school in the community, and a residential setting, such as a state training school or "boot camp" where the adolescent is removed from the community. Many treatment approaches, for example educational and vocational training, could readily be applied in either a residential or community setting.

What is clearly lacking is a standardized approach to treating antisocial behavior. The treatment that an antisocial adolescent receives may depend on what is available in the area, the predilections and theoretical orientation of the program administrators, financial constraints, etc. rather than on the particular needs of the adolescent. Effective treatments and prevention programs need to address what is understood about the causes of antisocial behavior. They need to be adequately evaluated and demonstrate their effectiveness through replication in various settings. This requirement is similar to what is expected of a new drug or medical device or technique. Interventions, whether legal or psychological, need to be based on evidence. Unfortunately, too often they are not. Below I present some examples of evidence-based programs that have been most successful in reducing antisocial behavior in conduct-disordered adolescents. Many of the programs I describe here and in the next chapter on prevention have been included in the Blue Prints for Violence Prevention project at the University of Colorado (*Juvenile Justice Bulletin,* July 2001, retrieved from www.ojjdp.ncjrs.org). In order to be included in the project the programs need to be proven effective in multiple settings. Only relatively few programs meet this standard. (These examples are not comprehensive. The reader interested in learning more about other effective treatment interventions can consult one of the recommended sources listed at the end of the book. The web site of the Office of Juvenile Justice and Delinquency Prevention is particularly helpful in this area.)

Many of the treatment approaches I describe in this chapter have been used to prevent the escalation of behavior problems in children as well as to mitigate the behavior problems of adolescents who have already been identified by the courts as delinquents. Whether an intervention is identified as a treatment or prevention depends on the age of the child when the intervention is applied and how far along the behavior problem has progressed. Programs designed to help families of very young children are clearly prevention programs. However, a treatment, such as those that work with families (some of which I describe below), might be applied to a family of an elementary-school child, in which case it might be labeled as a prevention program; if applied to the family of an adolescent who has broken the law a number of times it could be described as a treatment intervention. Regardless of how they are labeled, most of the evidence-based programs intervene in three fundamental areas of the child's life: family, school, and the ways in which he or she perceives and responds to the social environment.

Working with Families

Taking their cue from systems theory and the research on delinquency—which has strongly suggested for close to one hundred years that many the causes for delinquency lie within the adolescent's family and environment—a number of treatment programs have been designed to intervene with the families and other aspects of the lives of delinquent adolescents. These interventions assume that improved communications with the family, a less coercive relationship between adolescent and parents, more positive feedback from the parents, and clearer expectations and greater consistency would benefit the adolescent and lead to reduced antisocial behavior.

One approach, developed by psychologist Gerald Patterson at the Oregon Social Learning Center, has received considerable attention. Known as parent management training (PMT), it is based on behavior modification principles (Patterson, Capaldi, and Bank, 1991). PMT refers to a variety of approaches which work primarily with parents to improve their skills in guiding and disciplining their children. Research has consistently found that harsh or inconsistent discipline frequently leads to behavior problems in children. Therapists meet with the parent(s) and help them to identify problematic behaviors and to establish appropriate and reasonable goals. For example, the child might be told: "When you are feeling angry you can talk to me about it, but you can't hit your little brother"; or, "You have to show me that you've finished your school homework before you can watch television." Patterson and his colleagues believe that parents and children tend to become involved in what they referred to as coercive relationships, in which the interaction between the child or adolescent and the parent is characterized by negativity. Parents pay attention to the child when he or she is behaving badly, and appropriate behaviors are frequently ignored. The parent might punish the child for fighting with his brother but ignore the times when he was trying to be helpful, thus inadvertently reinforcing the aggressive behavior through negative attention. In PMT parents are taught how to develop clear behavioral expectations and how to apply the principles of behavior modification by consistently responding positively to the desired behaviors and at the same time ignoring or using mild punishment, such as a loss of a privilege, for negative behavior. Parents meet regularly with the therapist to discuss progress and problems until such time as the desirable behaviors are well established.

On the other hand, children may have multiple difficulties, some of which exist outside the home, such as academic or peer-relationship problems. Parents may suffer from problems as well, such as unemployment, substance abuse, or psychiatric problems. Issues relating to parent-child attachment may be improved through reduced conflict, but more intangible qualities of the relationship such as love and caring and showing affection cannot easily be addressed through behavior modification.

PMT is one of the more extensively evaluated treatment interventions for antisocial and conduct-disordered children and adolescents. It has proven to be a highly effective intervention, although it appears to be more effective with latency-age children (six to twelve years of age) and younger adolescents than with older adolescents, perhaps because parents generally have less control over their children as they get older (Kazdin, 2001).

Functional Family Therapy

Another approach that has proven to be useful in helping delinquents is functional family therapy (FFT) (Alexander and Parsons, 1982). Unlike individual therapies in which one individual is identified as the patient, family therapies see the family as a system of interacting members, each of whom generate particular behaviors in other members, sometimes for the good and sometimes not. Family therapy focuses on problems in communication among the members of the family and the roles that the members of the family play.

The family therapist might help the family learn how to negotiate rules and expectations, look for ways other than blaming a family member to solve problems, and learn how to listen to other family members more empathetically. All of this increases family cohesiveness. The family therapist will also help the family to create and implement appropriate long-term behavioral goals. FFT also makes use of the behavior modification techniques used in parent management training. The assumption of this therapy is that more effective communication, less blame, and more consistency will create a more stable and protective environment in which the adolescent will have less need to act out his problems in the form of antisocial behavior.

FFT is a short-term therapy, usually twelve to thirty-six one-hour weekly sessions. In the twenty-five years since its development, FFT has been shown to be effective in reducing re-offending. In one study, only about 20 percent of the adolescents who participated in the FFT study committed an offense, compared to 36 percent of the control group, during the year following treatment (Office of Juvenile Justice and Delinquency Prevention, 2001).

Working with the Individual

One of the more effective forms of therapy for depression in adults and adolescents is known as cognitive therapy. Based on the work of psychiatrist Aaron Beck, it assumes that depression results from the way in which individuals cognitively process events that impact them. According to Beck's theory, individuals become depressed when they consistently interpret events negatively. Cognitive therapy involves challenging these negative interpretations or cognitions and helps the patient to see alternative and more objective ways of understanding things (Beck, 1976).

The psychologist Kenneth Dodge and his colleagues assumed that similar cognitive distortions go on in the minds of aggressive children and adolescents (Dodge, Pettit, and Bates, 1997). They believed that these children are more likely to attribute hostility to other's intentions in neutral social situations than other children and that this would cause them to respond more aggressively. (See chapter 2 for a more complete discussion.) Problem-solving training teaches children alternate ways of perceiving and responding to various interpersonal situations. For example, instead of assigning hostile intentions to the person in the school hallway who has accidentally bumped into him, the adolescent learns how to reevaluate the situation and respond to it in an appropriate way, such as by ignoring it or simply saying "excuse me." In this treatment the therapist models correct behavior and uses feedback and praise to the adolescent for responding more positively. This type of intervention has proven to be effective in reducing aggressive behavior particularly in older children and adolescents (Kazdin, 2001).

Psychologist Alan Kazdin and his colleagues applied both cognitive problem-solving training and parent management training to a group of 97 children aged seven through thirteen and their families (Kazdin, Siegel, and Bass, 1992). Thus they focused both on the problematical behavior of the child and the problematical family environment in which the child was being raised. While approximately 25 percent of the families dropped out of treatment, the combination of these two treatments resulted in significantly improved behavior in the remaining children as rated by both their parents and their teachers, as well as reduced antisocial behavior and self-reported delinquency. Parents also reported reduced levels of stress. These changes in behavior were seen up to one year after the completion of the study. However, the authors caution that while the results were positive, it isn't clear how long the benefits of treatment would be maintained. It would be important to know for instance whether these changes in behavior held up through adolescence. It would also be of interest to know whether this combination of treatments would be as effective with a somewhat older population of children, particularly those who already had some contact with the law.

Multisystemic Therapy

Perhaps one of the most promising innovations in the treatment of young offenders is multisystemic therapy (MST), developed by Scott Henggeler and his colleagues (Henggeler, Shoenwald, Borduin, Rowlands, and Cunningham, 1998). This intervention assumes that adolescents and their families typically have multiple problems and are exposed to multiple risks. These problems exist within the adolescent's interaction with his family, school, and peers. Such assumptions are supported by a considerable amount of research.

Typically MST works with seriously antisocial adolescents between fourteen and sixteen years old who come from diverse ethnic backgrounds. They also frequently have problems with substance abuse as well as academic difficulties and antisocial peers, and are often living in single-parent families. The goals of MST are to reduce delinquent and other forms of antisocial behavior and to serve as an alternative to out-of-home placement or incarceration.

MST is based in part on the theoretical work of Uri Bronfenbrenner, who emphasized that the behavior of the individual could be understood only in the context of the environments in which the person existed. Using that framework, MST works to improve the functioning of the adolescent's family, adjust his relationship to school, and alter antisocial peer relationships.

MST is an intensive intervention. Treatment teams, typically consisting of three counselors, are available to the family twenty-four hours a day seven days a week. Services are provided in the family's home at times that are convenient for them. This has the effect of reducing family resistance to treatment as well as reducing attrition rates. The average length of treatment is approximately sixty contact hours over a four-month period. Therapists work to improve the parent or guardian's discipline practices, improve family relationships and family support networks, decrease the adolescent's association with antisocial peers, and improve academic performance. The intervention is pragmatic and uses of a variety of cognitive, behavioral, and family treatment as needed.

Evaluations of MST have been quite positive. For example, in one study comparing seriously delinquent adolescents who received MST to a control group who received usual probation services showed that, fifty-nine weeks after they were referred for treatment, the group who received MST had significantly fewer arrests (.87 versus 1.52), less time incarcerated (5.8 weeks versus 16.2 weeks), and lower rates of self-reported delinquency (2.9 offenses versus 8.6 offenses). The families reported greater degrees of cohesion, and adolescents who received treatment reported lower levels of involvement in peer aggression (Hengeller, Melton, and Smith, 1992).

MST is currently being tried as an alternative to incarceration for adolescents in New York City under a project funded by the Vera Institute for Justice. The program will be evaluated for a period of three years. The current cost estimates of incarcerating an inmate in New York City is approximately $59,000 per year (with insurance and medical care the figure is closer to $100,000) compared with a cost of approximately $4,500 per family for MST (von Zielbauer, 2004, 1). Even with a failure rate of 30 percent, there is still a significant savings, and the adolescents and their families benefit considerably more from MST than incarceration. (For a further discussion of cost/benefits with regard to treatment and prevention see below.)

Multidimensional Treatment Foster Care

Multidimensional treatment foster care (MTFC) is another program which has been identified as an effective intervention by the Center for Violence Prevention in Boulder, Colorado. The program, developed by Patricia Chamberlain and her colleagues at the Oregon Social Learning Center in Eugene, Oregon, is designed to work with adolescent boys between twelve and seventeen years old who have histories of serious delinquent behavior and have been mandated by the court to be placed out of their homes (Fisher and Chamberlain, 2000). Like MST, MTFC is based on the assumption that families are the primary socialization agents of young people. However, in this instance the adolescents are removed from their biological families and temporarily placed in the care of carefully selected foster families.

The foster parents receive twenty hours of pre-service training in which they learn to analyze behavior and to implement an individualized behavior management program. The behavior management program within the foster home clearly specifies to the adolescent a set of expectations about behavior and a schedule of activities, e.g., getting up at a certain time, getting to school, completing homework assignments, etc. The points that the boys earn for meeting these expectations serve as reinforcements and can be traded for privileges on the following day. There is an emphasis within the foster family setting of reinforcing positive, prosocial behavior and achievements. Points are lost for rule infractions and negative behaviors. Emphasis is also placed on reducing contact with delinquent peers, since antisocial peer relationships have been identified as a major factor is maintaining delinquent behavior. The boys also participate in weekly individual therapy sessions which focus on problem solving, social skills training, and effective ways to manage anger. Boys progress through three levels of development until such time as they are allowed to participate in community activities without adult supervision. Foster families receive intensive support from trained staff through daily phone contact and weekly meetings.

While the adolescent is living with his foster family a family therapist works with his biological family in order to help them with the boy's eventual return. The family therapist provides the natural parents with management techniques which emphasize supporting their son's positive behavior, giving clear and consistent discipline, and providing close supervision. Boys are then gradually reintroduced into their original homes. The family therapist continues to provide support for about another three months. The average length of a boy's involvement in the program is six to nine months.

The results of the MTFC intervention have been encouraging. Fewer of the boys who were placed in MTFC homes ran away from their placements (30 percent versus 58 percent) and more of them ultimately completed the program (73 percent versus 36 percent) than boys who were assigned to traditional group care settings. Most importantly, one year after completing the program the MTFC boys were significantly less involved in antisocial behavior than the adolescents who did not participate in the program. For a period of one year after living with their foster families they had less official contact with the police and the courts (2.6 contacts versus 5.4 contacts) and less self-disclosed delinquent behavior (13 self-disclosed criminal activities versus 29 self-disclosed criminal activities) (Chamberlain and Reid, 1998).

Each of these treatments has shown positive results, and the majority of the adolescents who received these treatments showed reduced delinquent behaviors in comparison to control groups. Nonetheless, a significant number continued to engage in antisocial behavior. Boys who participated in MST and MTFC continued to have contact with the police and continued to self-report delinquent behavior at a higher rate than the general population of adolescents, even though it was significantly lower than the rates of those boys who did not receive these treatments. Perhaps it is unreasonable to expect that any single intervention, no matter how well designed, could completely eliminate the antisocial behavior that has been developing in these boys over the course of their lifetimes. Many continue to live in impoverished neighborhoods with high crime rates. Longer term follow-ups, perhaps up to ten years post-treatment, would give us a clearer sense of whether the program participants continued to improve.

One of the problems with research in psychology is that it is so specialized that it often becomes parochial. In this instance, the writers in the field of delinquency treatment do not refer to the extensive research which has been conducted on psychotherapy with adults or non-delinquent adolescents. This research would suggest that there may be common factors that are affecting the outcome of these treatments, such as the motivation of the families, their feelings about the therapist, the opportunity to gain a new perspective on their problems, and perhaps something as simple as the fact that someone cares enough about them to pay attention to their difficulties. The same would hold true for individual therapies with delinquent adolescents.

Other difficulties include the fact that many of these families have multiple psychosocial problems, including parents' psychopathology such as depression or substance abuse, unemployment, financial difficulties, marital problems, etc. This often is related to families dropping out of treatment. Parent-child bonding may also be an issue. Anger or disinterest on the part of the parent would most certainly affect the outcome. Most seriously delinquent teens come from seriously problematical families, so therapy must address not only the adolescent's problems but those of his parents as well. In fact, anything that affects the parent(s) will impact the adolescent. One of the strengths of MST is that it addresses many of these issues, but in reality, many of the problems are so complex that it is difficult to see how they could be adequately addressed and resolved in three to six months.

While it is encouraging to see that treatment programs for serious juvenile offenders can be effective, there are a number of significant questions that remain unanswered. First, why is there such a large percentage of adolescents who do not respond to treatment? The research data provide by Lipsey and Wilson suggest that even in the best of programs some 30 percent of youths still continue to re-offend. This is still a very significant percentage. How do those who succeed differ from those who do not? And what do we do with those who did not benefit from the intervention?

Secondly, since we are working with individuals who have a large part of their lives ahead of them (most, after all, are only about sixteen years old or younger), we might also be interested to learn about the quality of lives that they lead afterward, even if they don't commit any further offenses. (Treatment response is measured in terms of re-offending.) Do they finish school? Do they get vocational training, learn a trade, go to college? What kind of marriages do they have? Are those marriages stable? What kind of parents do they become? Are they concerned with their children's education and well-being? Do they make a contribution to their communities—for example, coach the kid's basketball teams or little league? Do they have friends or are they isolated? Do they vote? Are they happy or do they suffer from anxiety or depressive disorders? Do they become substance abusers? Are they physically healthy? We need to remember that the large majority of the adolescents who wind up in these various treatment programs have not had very happy or successful childhoods. Their early lives have been marked by conflict, they come from dysfunctional families, have failed in school, live with the stresses associated with poverty, etc. To feel in the least bit sanguine about the fact that we can demonstrate statistically that they don't re-offend is to seriously miss the point. There is more to life than staying out of jail.

As mentioned in chapter 3, for the most part, the lives of serious adolescent offenders tend not to go well. Research in this area suggests that a significant percentage (30 to 50 percent) of severely antisocial children continue to exhibit antisocial behavior in adulthood (Robbins, 1978). Other problems include earlier sexual relationships, difficulties with interpersonal relationships, greater frequency of violent deaths, a greater number of psychiatric disorders including depression, a variety of anxiety disorders, and a higher rate of substance abuse problems (Maughn, 2001). This is not to say that all continue an antisocial or unhappy lifestyle. Some benefit from interventions in childhood or adolescence, others benefit from various protective factors such as a strong intellect or talent, or perhaps fortuitous life events such as marrying a strong and supportive partner, or acquiring a meaningful job. But the numbers who fail and suffer in their lives, even if they don't wind up in prison or in trouble with the law, is uncomfortably high.

Conclusions

This chapter has dealt with both judicial and psychological responses to antisocial behavior in adolescence. It would appear that little progress has been made in the judicial area since the establishment of the first juvenile court one hundred years ago. The juvenile court was established to rehabilitate and help juvenile offenders as opposed to punishing them. The court recognized at that time that adolescents required a more tempered response to their behavior. However, over the past hundred years the sense of the public as well as state legislators was that the courts were failing in their mission to rehabilitate and control the problem of antisocial behavior in adolescents and more punitive responses to delinquency were instituted.

The problem has been and still is that juvenile justice legislation has not been affected by social science research, which has suggested that adolescents should not be held accountable in the same way as adults and that more punitive response are not necessarily more effective deterrents. Furthermore, the lack of consistent responses to similar behavior from one jurisdiction to another and from one state to another suggests a lack of coherent and reasoned judicial policy. While some of these problems are being addressed, there still is a long way to go.

With regard to treatment interventions for CDAs the picture is somewhat brighter. The introduction of behavioral and cognitive techniques in treating adolescents has been quite successful. The advent of evidence-based treatments such as PMT and MST have been demonstrated to have a significant impact on the behavior of many antisocial adolescents. However, despite their effectiveness it may be too little too late. The success of these interventions is measured in terms of specific criteria such as degree of aggressiveness and number of arrests, detentions, and self-reported delinquent episodes. While program participants do better compared to nonparticipants on these measures, they still remain symptomatic; indeed, many might still meet the criteria for conduct disorder. It isn't at all clear that they have been returned to "normal" functioning. Furthermore, at present we know little about the long-term follow-up of the participants compared to their controls. For example, how different will they appear to be ten years later? It may be that without more extensive interventions into the lives of these adolescents, such as improving their housing and neighborhoods and providing significantly better educational and vocational opportunities, that the quality of their lives may not be appreciably improved.

5

Preventing Juvenile Delinquency

Prevention is better than cure.
Early-seventeenth-century proverb

According to the police report, two witnesses saw Freddie along with two other teenagers assault and rob another adolescent. Following this attack the witnesses stated that they observed the three boys approach another victim but didn't actually observe an attack in that instance. The first victim, who had apparently been drinking, ultimately died from his injuries. Freddie admitted to attacking the victim but denied that robbery was the motive. He said that the attack was motivated by revenge, a "payback" for an attack on another youth. He was charged with felony murder. Freddie had prior juvenile offenses. When he was ten years old he had broken into his elementary school with a group of other juveniles, and the following year a complaint had been filed against him for shoplifting. The year prior to his current offense he was charged with assaulting another juvenile.

Freddie lives with his mother and three other siblings, of which he is the next-to-oldest child. Freddie's father was in jail. Freddie told the psychologist that examined him that he was in the eighth grade and that he had repeated the seventh grade due to excessive absences. He said he would stay out late at night and then not go to school the next day. He had been suspended from school in the fourth grade as a result of his defiant behavior.

Psychological testing found Freddie to be of normal intelligence with no signs of serious psychiatric disorders. He said that he did not use alcohol or drugs. While he first denied family problems, he later admitted to arguing and fighting a lot with his mother. He hadn't seen his father in several years. His mother reported that he had been a "difficult child" and hard to discipline ever since he was a toddler.

If we had observed Freddie as a small boy doing the mugging in our hypothetical sandbox, as described in chapter 2, we would have been very concerned as to whether his antisocial behavior would continue into his adolescence. If we believed the likelihood was high that this behavior would continue, we would have wanted to intervene in his life in some way so as to alter this unhappy outcome. Probably the best predictor of whether he would act in this way would be the continuation of this antisocial behavior as he aged. If he continued his sandbox muggings into preschool, and if his sandbox muggings became schoolyard muggings in elementary school, then there would be a significant probability that he would continue this sort of behavior into adolescence. The longer Freddie's aggressive behavior continued during childhood, the greater the likelihood it would continue. A study by psychologist Gerald Patterson and his colleagues found that half the boys who were rated as most aggressive by their teachers and peers in the second grade (age 8) were arrested by the time they were in the ninth grade, compared to only 7 percent of those who were not rated as aggressive (Patterson, Capaldi, and Bank, 1991). Certainly it would have been better for Freddie and everyone else concerned to have been able to alter his behavior prior to his beginning his delinquent career.

In the last chapter I noted that the surgeon general of the United States, Dr. David Satcher, issued a report in which he identified youth violence as a public health concern. The introduction to the report suggests that the emphasis in responding to the problem of serious delinquency should be on prevention, as opposed to rehabilitation. There are a number of good reasons for this. First, one of the major problems associated with treatment interventions for serious juvenile offenders is that they occur relatively late in youngsters' lives. By the time the intervention occurs, even if it is as early as ten years old, the child has typically experienced a considerable degree of unhappiness and failure in life. Children deserve better, and it is in fact possible to provide them with considerably more help than they get. Second, because it is difficult to make up for a lost childhood, prevention in early childhood can have a greater and more meaningful effect than intervention during adolescence. The longer a problematic behavior exists, the more difficult it is to change. Acute problems are easier to respond to than chronic ones. Third, primary prevention interventions are usually more cost effective than treatment interventions. It costs much less to educate primary and middle-school children about the health hazards associated with smoking cigarettes than it is to treat lung cancer and heart disease. It is more efficient to help a young child of six, along with his family, with a behavior problem than it is to try to treat him in a residential treatment facility at age fifteen.

A public-health approach typically operates by defining the nature of the problem; describing how frequently the disorder or disease occurs and how widespread it is through the population; identifying potential causes as well as risk and protective factors associated with the disorder; developing and evaluating specific interventions; and educating the public. Using this approach, individuals who are at risk for developing a particular disorder can be identified. Just as individuals who engage in unprotected sex and have multiple sex partners are at higher risk for contracting AIDS, male children who are raised in poverty, who have aggressive dispositions, and who come from disorganized families are at greater risk for becoming delinquent as adolescents. Once the risk factors associated with a particular disorder are identified, it becomes possible to develop strategies to respond to a problem. Strategies which are designed to prevent the occurrence of the disorder in the first place are referred to as primary prevention. For example, educating drug addicts about the dangers involved in sharing needles and providing them with a supply of clean needles can prevent the spread of AIDS, just as providing social and psychological support to the families of children living in poverty can decrease the likelihood of those children becoming delinquent or developing other mental health problems. Clearly it is more reasonable to provide AIDS education and sterile syringes to an at-risk population than it is to treat AIDS once it occurs. In the same vein, it is more reasonable to provide support to families and young children at risk early on, compared to the costs involved in prosecuting and incarcerating delinquent adolescents.

Predicting Serious Juvenile Delinquency

The risk factors associated with delinquency (as identified in chapters 2 and 3) vary in terms of their effectiveness in predicting later delinquent behavior. For example, having a biological parent with a history of criminal behavior is a stronger predictor of later delinquent behavior than coming from a single-parent home. Research studies which identify risk factors or predictors can be done either prospectively, as in longitudinal studies, or retrospectively, by collecting information from and about a known population of delinquents. The researchers need to decide upon appropriate criteria for delinquent behavior. These might be based on official arrest records, court records, or self-reported delinquent behavior—or a combination of these. The choice of criteria is quite important since adolescents may engage in a significant amount of antisocial behavior which is not brought to the attention of the police or juvenile court.

Good predictors at one age may not be good predictors at another. Aggressive behavior in preschool may not be a good predictor of adolescent violence, but aggressive behavior at age ten may be a very good predictor. Alternately, substance abuse is a good predictor of later antisocial behavior when noted in late childhood but not when noted in early adolescence. Also, identifying single predictors may not present an accurate picture without understanding other factors which may exacerbate, or in some instances mitigate, the likelihood of later delinquent behavior. For instance, being raised in an impoverished environment may be a strong predictor of later delinquent behavior, but at the same time, being raised in a stable home may mitigate the effects of poverty. (See discussion of protective factors in chapter 2.) Thus, accurately predicting and understanding outcomes may depend on a number of measures which would need to be taken simultaneously at one point in time, whereas other measures might need to be gathered at another point in the child's life.

All of these issues make prediction a rather difficult proposition. While it can be done with more certainty than predicting the winner of a horse race, it still involves fortune-telling. Nonetheless, in looking at the studies which have attempted to develop predictors, there is a large degree of correlation. These overlapping results provide a certain measure of confidence in the results, since different researchers using different measurement techniques and working with different populations are finding similar results.

One of the first large-scale review studies of predictors of delinquency was conducted by researchers Rolf Loeber and Thomas Dishion in 1983. Loeber and Dishion analyzed the results of sixty studies which examined the relationship between several variables, including the child's behavior, academic performance, family size and functioning, and serious delinquent behavior in adolescence. They found that the best predictor of antisocial behavior in adolescence was a composite measure of parental family management techniques. This would be defined as a combination of how children were disciplined and rewarded, the consistency of consequences, etc. The second best predictor was aggressive behavior in childhood, as reported by teachers, parents, or peers. A history of stealing, lying, or truancy was the third most effective predictor, followed by criminality or antisocial behavior of family members, and then poor educational achievement.

More recent syntheses of predictors of delinquent behavior have been conducted by J. David Hawkins and his colleagues (Hawkins, Herrenkohl, Farrington, Brewer, Catalano, and Harachi, 1998) and Mark Lipsey and James Derzon (1998). These researchers determined the "odds ratio" of a particular variable predicting serious antisocial behavior, including violence, later in life. The odds ratio is the likelihood of an antisocial or violent individual's having a particular risk factor divided by the likelihood of exhibiting this type of behavior without the presence of the risk factor. The researchers determined these odds ratios by re-analyzing the data of a large number of studies. For example, in re-analyzing studies that examined children's attitudes and beliefs they noted that for peer-rated dishonesty at age ten, the odds ratio associated with violent crime convictions between the ages of ten and thirty-two was 9.0. This means that, based on the data collected from the children who participated in this study, children who were rated as dishonest by their peers were nine times more likely to be convicted of a violent offense. The data from another study found that children between the ages of five and fifteen whose parents reported that they were stealing were almost twelve times more likely to be convicted of a violent offense between the ages of twenty and thirty than children whose parents did not report this behavior (an odds ratio of 12).

The findings of both Hawkins and his colleagues and Lipsey and Derzon are consistent. The strongest predictors for children between the ages of six and eleven are being male, early indications of antisocial behavior (which include actual offenses and aggressive behavior), having antisocial parents, problematic family relationships, and being poor. Other important predictors include poor school performance and having antisocial peers, particularly in adolescence.

It's not surprising that one of the better predictors of antisocial behavior in adolescence is antisocial behavior in childhood, since we would expect that by age eight or nine a child would have developed sufficient internal controls to be able to inhibit his aggressiveness and have mastered prosocial skills for dealing with frustration and conflict. A diagnosis of moderate to severe conduct disorder in childhood does not bode well for behavior in adolescence, unless adequate steps are taken to intervene.

A large number of studies have demonstrated that, while not always the case, aggressive behavior, particularly that noted in the primary grades by teachers, parents, and peers, tends to be relatively stable and often persists well into early adulthood (Olweus, 1979). From a practical point of view it is important to correctly identify the children in a given population who will become delinquent and at the same time not falsely classify children as potential delinquents. The difficulty of this task is represented in table 5.1. In this hypothetical example, I have used poor maternal attachment at age five as rated by a psychologist as a predictor of later delinquent behavior. Represented here are ninety children out of a population of one thousand identified as having this poor attachment. Let's say that when the court records of all one thousand were examined when the children were fifteen years of age, a total of one hundred were adjudicated as delinquent by the court. The quality of maternal attachment correctly identified sixty (or 60 percent) of the hundred children who were adjudicated. However, it also misidentified thirty children who did not later become delinquent. These are referred to as false positives. The use of this criterion

Table 5.1. Use of a Hypothetical Risk Factor for Predicting Delinquent Outcomes

	Adjudicated	Not adjudicated	Adjudicated and not adjudicated
Poor maternal attachment	Valid positives 60	False positives 30	
Good maternal attachment	False negatives 40	Valid negatives 870	
Totals	100	900	1,000

also missed forty children who did become delinquent. The quality of maternal attachment also correctly predicted 870 of the 910 children who would not be adjudicated by age fifteen. A prevention program that was implemented for the ninety children with poor maternal attachment would reach sixty children who would become delinquent and treat thirty who would not. There would also be forty children who would not receive services who would actually benefit from it (the false negatives).

It is possible to improve accuracy by using multiple criteria, for example by combining ratings of maternal attachment and teachers' ratings of classroom behavior in the first grade. Sometimes these criteria may be used sequentially. For example, teachers' ratings might first be obtained and then information may be gathered from the parents for those who are identified as having behavior problems; then for those identified by both parents and teachers an individual evaluation might be conducted by a mental health professional. This technique, known as "gating," is a more cost effective way of obtaining predictive information about a child. However, no criterion (single or multiple) is perfect. Furthermore, as noted earlier, predictors are not static. What might be a good predictor of adolescent delinquent behavior at age eight might not be a good predictor at age twelve. Lipsey and Derzon found that substance abuse (use) between the ages of six and eleven was a strong predictor of later serious delinquency, but substance use between ages twelve and fourteen was not. This makes sense, since the frequency of substance use among six to eleven year olds is relatively rare, thus more indicative of serious problems, whereas substance abuse among twelve to fourteen year olds is much more pervasive.

Other factors that affect the accuracy of predictors are the outcome criteria that are used. In our hypothetical example, the outcome criterion was adjudication by the court by age fifteen, an official measure of delinquency. If self-reported serious delinquent behavior (an unofficial measure of delinquency which tends to pick up a greater frequency of delinquent acts) was used, the number of valid positives, false positives, and false negatives would change. Prediction is not an easy task.

Predictors are usually seen in terms of a cost benefit analysis— that is, comparing the costs involved in providing services to children who will not become delinquent (the false positives) to the costs involved in not providing services to children who would potentially benefit (the false negatives). One of the problems associated with focusing on predictors of serious and violent delinquent behavior as a sole outcome criterion on which to base intervention programs is that it excludes children who may have negative outcomes other than serious delinquency in adolescence. Even though having neglectful and/or abusive parents may not be a strong predictor of serious and violent behavior in adolescence, it may be a strong predictor of substance abuse, academic failure, depression, poor parenting in adulthood, and other problems. Attending only to whether or not a particular variable or group of variables can accurately predict antisocial behavior in adolescence is buying into society's need for reduced antisocial behavior in adolescence, which is quite legitimate, but at the same time it is ignoring the more pervasive needs of children. Preventing unhappiness and failure in adolescence is also an important goal, whether or not that unhappiness and failure expresses itself in the form of antisocial behavior.

Preventing Juvenile Delinquency

In his foreword, entitled "Never too Early," to the collection *Serious and Violent Offenders,* James Q. Wilson, the Harvard professor of government and public policy and coauthor of the well-received book *Crime and Human Nature* (1998), notes the importance of early childhood experiences and constitutional factors in explaining why some children become seriously antisocial during their adolescent years. He emphasizes the importance of early interventions with the child and his or her family. While this foreword was written in 1998, this is a fact that has been known by researchers in the field for a very long time. It is not news, but rather an issue which has come to the forefront repeatedly. As we have seen, one of the best predictors of antisocial behavior in adolescence is antisocial behavior in childhood, which means that the child, his teachers, and his family are already having a problem early in the child's life. True primary prevention programs would focus on preventing the precursors to antisocial behavior in childhood, such as poor school performance, problematic behavior at home and in school, and poor family functioning.

Prevention programs need to address those factors which put the child at risk for developing behavioral or other problems later in life. I have suggested that these factors are complex and interact with each other. For example, the child's temperament interacts with the way in which discipline is handled within his family. To be truly effective, early interventions need to take into account the child's stage of development, his or her strengths and weaknesses, the family context in which the child is being raised, the school and neighborhood, etc. Programs that do not address validated risks associated with conduct disorder in childhood and adolescence are less likely to succeed.

Programs which engage a broad population of children who are at some moderate degree of risk are referred to as *universal* programs. A pre-kindergarten program for all children living below a certain income level is an example of a universal program. We know that poverty is frequently associated with poor school performance, which is in turn later related to antisocial behavior. A pre-kindergarten program increases the likelihood of better school performance and over time reduces the likelihood of antisocial behavior. Universal programs are cost efficient on a per-child basis, and no child within the program is labeled as having a problem. There are fewer stigmas associated with participating in a universal program.

Selected programs are designed to help a subgroup of children who are at a still higher level of risk. For example, a special program might be developed within the pre-kindergarten curriculum for children whom the teachers have identified as particularly aggressive. On the other hand, the risk might not necessarily exist within the child; it might lie within the child's family. For instance, knowing that the parents of the child are substance abusers or under a high level of stress might indicate the need for additional services for the child and his family.

Indicated programs are for those children who show even more problematic behavior and might meet some of the criteria for conduct disorder and who are perceived to be at the highest risk for developing serious behavior problems. Indicated programs are likely to be more intense and more costly, at least on a short-term basis, than universal interventions.

Terminology aside, an effective prevention program is one that will provide a reasonably good environment (including the child's family), respond to his or her developmental and educational needs, and address any special problems he or she might have such as a learning disability or ADHD.

Prevention Programs with Pregnant Mothers and Infants

Anyone who has any contact with babies and small children knows how fragile, needy, vulnerable, and demanding they are. The world they live in is one which is created by their caretaker(s), usually the mother, whose job it is to provide a safe, loving environment. The child analyst Donald Winnicott (1960) talked about the mother providing a "holding environment" for the infant in which its physical and emotional needs are responded to. The mother is able to provide for the baby through her empathetic understanding of her child's needs. While much of this cannot be easily quantified, "good mothering" in infancy is more likely to lead to secure attachment. There are a number of studies, some of which I have described in chapter 2, which point to the importance of the early relationship between mother and child in all areas of the child's development, including appropriate behavior.

In recognition of the importance of this earliest of relationships, a number of primary prevention programs have been directed at providing support for mothers both during their pregnancy and then during the child's early years. Winnicott states: "It should be noted that mothers who have it in them to provide good-enough care can be enabled to do better by being cared for themselves in a way that acknowledges the essential nature of their task" (Winnicott, 1960). These programs cannot be thought of as delinquency-prevention programs, but the fact that they are designed to provide for a more secure environment for the infant and young child may in fact prevent other problematic behaviors, such as school failure, substance abuse, and various other psychological disorders. These programs basically attempt to provide these children with mothers who can take care of them in a reasonable and sensitive way. This is far removed from the juvenile justice system and falls more under the rubric of child welfare, yet the research I described in earlier chapters has repeatedly pointed out the connection between early childhood experiences and antisocial behavior in adolescence.

One such program for pregnant women was the Elmira Home Visitation project in Elmira, New York (Olds, Eckenrode, and Henderson, 1997). Participants in this program were selected if they met any of the following criteria: the mother to be was younger than nineteen, unmarried, or of low socioeconomic status (Olds, Henderson, and Cole, 1998). The women were provided with transportation for prenatal care and well-baby care for the first two years of the child's life. They also received home visits from a nurse during this period of time. The nurses supported the mother's health care, early childhood parenting, and the mother's personal development.

The outcomes of this program were quite positive. The smokers who participated in the program had fewer premature deliveries and had babies who weighed more than did the control group. The mothers as a group were less likely to abuse or neglect their children, and based on the nurses' observations, were less likely to punish or restrict their children. The supported mothers had fewer subsequent pregnancies and waited a longer period of time before becoming pregnant again than did the control group of mothers. They relied less on public welfare and were more likely to return to school and be employed. The mothers who participated in the program reported less alcohol and drug abuse and had fewer arrests. When followed up fifteen years later, the children of the unmarried, low-socioeconomic-status mothers reported fewer arrests and fewer conviction and parole violations, although there were no differences between the treatment and control group children in teacher ratings of acting-out behavior in school.

The Syracuse University Family Development Research Program was similar in many ways to the one in Elmira. This program provided various services to low-income mothers during the last trimester of their pregnancy and continued through the first five years of the children's lives (Lally, Mangione, and Honig, 1998). Mothers received weekly visits at home from paraprofessionals who provided assistance with parenting and family issues, as well as helping with employment. The program also provided half-time day care for the first fifteen months of the child's life and full-time day care through age five. Compared to the control group, younger children functioned at a higher cognitive and social and emotional level. Older children in the intervention group had significantly lower rates of convictions for juvenile delinquency, and reported less chronic delinquent behavior.

A third program that had positive results was the Yale Child Welfare Research Program (Seitz, Rosenbaum, and Apfel, 1985). This program provided assistance to a small group of poor women (seventeen) who were pregnant with their first child until the toddler was two and half. Services included home visits by health professionals who helped the mothers with various problems in living, such as obtaining adequate housing and making educational and career decisions. Health care services were provided for the children. Mothers were provided with information about child development and were free to discuss child-rearing problems. Day care was provided for the children between the ages of two to twenty-eight months. When followed up ten years later, these families were more likely to be self-supporting and mothers had fewer and more widely spaced babies. The mothers were more likely to be involved with their children's education. Thus, children had better school attendance and adjustment than the control group. The boys of mothers in the program were better behaved in school.

One of the significant advantages of becoming involved with women during their pregnancy is that it increases the likelihood the baby will be normal and healthy at birth. Nurses and paraprofessionals can counsel the expectant mothers regarding proper nutrition and the dangers associated with alcohol and smoking to their unborn babies. The nurses can also be available immediately after the baby is born, typically a period of stress for single mothers who may otherwise have little assistance with their newborns. While evidence is lacking in this area, this extra help probably also assures a better "bonding" between mother and baby and allows the new mother to provide a more secure emotional environment for her child. This is a reasonable birthright for all children. Providing these mothers with help with their parenting skills helps the mother and child get off to a good start. Many of these mothers did not experience good parenting themselves, and often have not had an adequate role model for their own mothering behavior.

One explanation for the positive impact of these programs has been called the "snowball effect," referring to the fact that positive experiences early in life are more likely to lead to positive experiences later on (Zigler, Taussig, and Black, 1992). Children who feel secure in their relationship to their caretakers are less likely to act out in preschool, and thus get more positive feedback from their teachers. This in turn increases their attachment to school and so on.

Prevention Programs for Preschool Children

Intervening with children and their families early in their lives has distinct advantages over later interventions. Young children are much more flexible than are older children; problematic behaviors have not yet become habitual; and children have not yet been labeled as "bad" by teachers and parents. Getting children off to a good start in school has enormous benefits; school will more likely be a positive experience and they will be more likely to learn and develop good peer relationships, thus strengthening protective factors which have been shown to reduce the likelihood of antisocial behavior in adolescence.

There have been a number of programs which have successfully addressed the needs of preschool children. One of the more widely discussed programs was the Perry Preschool Project (Berruta-Clement, Schweinhart, Barnett, and Weikart, 1987). This program involved fifty-eight three- and four-year-old children who were at risk for school failure due to low intellectual functioning. Most of the children were from poor black families. Less than one in five of the parents of these children had completed high school, and half of the families were receiving welfare assistance. The children attended the preschool for two years for two and half hours a day, five days a week. In addition, teachers visited the mothers and children at home for one and one half hours a week. In their adolescence, the children who attended preschool had fewer arrests and were less likely to be involved in a serious fight. Overall, they were less often involved with the police. Of equal importance was the fact that children who attended the preschool were more likely to graduate from high school and get some form of vocational training. They were less likely to be on welfare, and the girls who attended the program were less likely to become pregnant during their adolescence. The authors of the study suggest that positive early schooling experiences lead to greater school success and educational achievement later on. Another intervention designed to prevent conduct problems and promote social competence in young children is known as the Incredible Years Parent, Teacher, and Child Training Series. In one recent study Carolyn Webster-Stratton and her colleagues at the school of nursing at the University of Washington in Seattle worked with 272 mothers of four-year-old children in Head Start programs as well as 61 of the teachers (Webster-Stratton, Reid, and Hammond, 2001). The twelve-week parent training program covered topics such as playing with your child, helping your child to learn, and effective parent management skills like limit setting and handling misbehavior. Follow-up sessions included discussions on facilitating friendships, interactive reading with children, problem solving, and working with teachers. Parents viewed brief video tapes which modeled positive parenting, followed by a discussion led by a trained leader.

The teacher training aspect of the program focused on positive classroom management, discipline strategies, and developing social competency in children. Teachers attended six one-day-a-month sessions. During each session the teachers viewed a brief video tape, followed by a discussion on topics including developing positive relationships with students and families, improving children's social skills, effective ways of responding to misbehavior, teaching anger management, working with parents, and helping the children to express feelings.

The researchers reported positive outcomes as a result of these interventions. The parents of the children showed increased positive parenting style, reduced harsh discipline, and improved "bonding" compared to mothers who did not participate in the programs. The children themselves showed significantly fewer conduct problems at school in one-year follow-ups. Indeed, 80 percent of the children identified as being at "high risk" for future behavior problems moved into the low risk category, compared to 48 percent of the control group children.

One question that is frequently not addressed is what are the factors that prevent the parents of these children from interacting effectively with their children in the first place? Is it stress, poverty, personal problems, or their own negative experiences with being parented themselves? Most parents effectively discipline, praise, play with, teach, and interact with their children in a positive and caring manner without participating in training programs. Are these parenting problems that are passed down from one generation to the next? If so, perhaps interventions which teach parenting skills should take place before young people have children.

Another aspect of the Incredible Years Series is a treatment program for children showing early signs of conduct disorder (Webster-Stratton and Reid, 2003). The intervention, known as the "Dina Dinosaur" program, works with children from four to eight years of age (preschool through second grade). The authors point out that intervening with behavior problems early in the child's life, when they more malleable, prevents the problems from crystallizing and helps the child to benefit from improved interpersonal relationships during the elementary school years. The program, based on research on the causes of conduct disorder in young children, teaches the participants how to understand their feelings, how to deal with interpersonal conflicts and problems, and how to manage their angry feelings. Children meet in small groups weekly for two hours over an eighteen-to-twenty-week period. The groups utilize child-friendly techniques such as video tapes, puppets, and games.

Children who participated in the program showed significant improvements in peer interactions when compared to a parent training only condition (described above) or the control group. However, the most effective intervention was using both the parent training and the child training programs. Ninety-five percent of the children who participated in the Dina Dinosaur program while their parents participated in the parent training program continued to show improved behavior one year after they had completed the program. In addition, adding the teacher training condition had positive effects on classroom behavior. The Incredible Years Series has been adopted by numerous agencies in the United States as well as Canada, the United Kingdom, Norway, and Australia.

Prevention Programs for Elementary School Children

The next logical place to implement prevention programs is in the elementary schools. There are both theoretical and practical reasons for this. Most seriously delinquent children have a history of school failure and perform at below grade level in basic subjects such as reading and mathematics. Secondly, conduct-disordered behaviors are likely to become most problematic in a school setting, where for the first time children are exposed to a more structured environment with clear behavioral expectations. Children at risk for more serious problems can be identified by teachers as early as kindergarten. As mentioned earlier, one of the better predictors of later delinquency is teachers' ratings of children's behavior problems in the early school years.

Schools themselves are the most important socialization agents that young children are exposed to outside of their families, and so play a very important role in the development of appropriate behavior. Young children are more malleable and more easily influenced by adults than are adolescents, who are more likely to be resistant and more susceptible to negative peer influence. From a practical point of view, all children must attend school, whereas not all children need to attend preschool; hence it is possible to have access to a whole population of children without having to recruit families.

One such program which had positive effects was the Seattle Social Development Project (Hawkins, Catalano, Kosterman, Abbot, and Hill, 1999; O'Donnel, Hawkins, Catalano, Abbot, and Day, 1995). This comprehensive program was implemented with children from the first through the fifth grade. Teachers were trained in classroom management techniques as well as in the use of behavior management to support positive behavior. Parents were offered parent management training courses to help them to deal with their children at home, and the children were provided with social competency training.

The outcomes were quite positive. By the second grade, boys who participated in the program were rated as less aggressive than those who did not. By the fifth grade participating students rated their family communication and involvement as better than the nonparticipants. Participants were more committed to school and saw school as more rewarding than the nonparticipants. Six years after completing the program, as adolescents, they remained more committed to school and they were better behaved and performed better academically in school than those who were not part of the program. Also of great importance was the fact that they self-reported less violent criminal behavior, heavy drinking, and pregnancies.

The FAST Track program is another primary prevention program which is aimed both at a school-wide population and at a subgroup of high-risk children who exhibit behavior problems. The program uses the PATHS curriculum (Promoting Alternative Thinking Strategies) in the classroom for all children. This curriculum focuses on four areas of social and emotional competence: teaching children to understand and communicate emotions and feelings effectively; teaching skills that relate to social interactions, such as making friends, taking turns, and sharing; teaching self-control; and teaching techniques for solving social problems. The parents of children who are identified as at high risk (based on parent and teacher ratings of aggressive behavior) were offered the opportunity to attend parent training groups. High-risk children were offered special social skills groups, academic tutoring, and after-school enrichment programs. One of the more interesting features of the program is that it is designed to be implemented from grades one through grade ten, thus providing extra support from childhood into the early stages of adolescence. This program, as are many other school-based programs, is posited on the assumption that children who get off to a good academic and social start in school are more likely to succeed and less likely to engage in delinquent behavior (Conduct Problems Research Prevention Group, 1999).

The initial results of the intervention have been positive. At the end of the first year, the children who participated in the program were better able to deal with social situations and could more readily verbalize their feelings compared to the children who were not part of the program. Parents who participated had warmer interactions with their children, punished them less harshly, were more consistent in their discipline, and were more involved with their children's school. Ratings of the children by observers, who were unaware whether or not the children were in the treatment group, supported the findings that the children who had taken part in the program had made significant improvements in terms of reduced disruptive behavior. These results are encouraging, given the fact that the program was working with the more problematic children in the school and children who lived in poor neighborhoods with high rates of crime.

The Montreal Prevention Experiment worked with boys between the ages of seven and nine who were identified by their teachers as being unusually disruptive (McCord, Tremblay, Vitaro, and Desmarais-Gervais, 1994). The program provided the boys with various types of social skills training, which included topics such as making friends, giving help, following rules, handling anger, etc. The parents of these boys were provided with parent management training, which I described in the previous chapter. The results were positive. At twelve years of age boys who had received help did better in school and reported less antisocial behavior than the boys in the control group. On the other hand, the improvements were small. While only 14 percent of the control group ultimately made a satisfactory adjustment to school, only 30 percent of the treatment group had made a satisfactory school adjustment. While the group differences are significant, that still left 70 percent of the treated group struggling.

Two other recently reported prevention programs were the Peace Builders Program implemented in Arizona and the Resolving Conflict Creatively Program in New York City (Flannery, 2003; Aber, Brown, and Jones, 2003). Both of these programs were conducted in elementary schools and were administered universally, that is, to all children in the schools. Both programs were designed to be part of the regular school curriculum and were taught by the teachers in the school. The Peace Builders Program focused on establishing a school-wide climate that supported prosocial behavior rather than just reducing negative behavior. In addition to classroom lessons on positive behavior, signs were placed around the school reminding the students about good behavior rules and principles. The New York City program was also school and classroom based and focused on teaching elementary school children more effective ways of dealing with conflicts and teaching self-respect as well as respect for others. While the programs differed in many respects, both were designed to decrease aggressive and negative behavior in elementary school children, while increasing more prosocial behavior through classroom education. Both programs reported success in this area, with teachers and the students themselves reporting less aggressive behavior and greater social competence. However, unlike the FAST Track Program, parents were not involved in the Resolving Conflicts Creatively program. These universal, school-based prevention programs are based on the assumption that it is easier to respond to behavior problems when the children are young and behavior patterns are not as firmly established as they might be in adolescence. On the other hand, there is not yet evidence from any of the elementary-school-based programs regarding their impact on delinquent behavior in adolescence.

Overall Evaluation of Prevention Programs

There is clear evidence that prenatal through infancy, preschool, and elementary-school prevention programs can be effective in reducing aggressive and antisocial behavior in children who are at risk. Further, by strengthening families and improving children's social competency, and in some instances academic skills, they also provide the children with protective factors which may remain with them through adolescence and adulthood. Some of these programs, such as the Perry Preschool Program, have shown an impact on adolescent behavior in terms of improved educational achievement and reduced delinquent behavior.

All of these interventions are primary prevention programs, since they are addressing the needs of children and their families *prior* to the onset of serious antisocial behavior. One of the important strengths of all of these programs is that they addressed specific risk factors associated with delinquency, including parenting problems, academic and social skills deficits, and early signs of aggressive behavior. Furthermore, they were all well evaluated, all but one making use of a treatment and control group. Programs of this sort are more likely to be funded in the future because they can empirically validate their success.

Another important benefit of these prevention programs is that they save taxpayer dollars. Steve Aos and his colleagues at the Washington State Institute for Public Policy conducted an analysis of several primary and secondary prevention programs which had been implemented in his state (Aos, Phipps, Bamoski, and Lieb, 2001). Program costs can be determined relatively precisely, since they include the staff, administrative, and capital expenses which make up the program's budget. Benefits are estimates based on the reduced costs involved in processing individuals through the criminal justice system, which would include court and incarceration costs. Aos also calculated benefits in terms of victims as well, taking account of lost work time, property loss, etc. There also may be less immediate benefit, as in the form of increased employment resulting in an increased tax role and reduced use of welfare services.

Table 5.2 presents some of the findings of Aos and his colleagues. The first column indicates the cost per program participant. For example, early childhood education programs cost about $8,900 per child. The second column indicates the savings to taxpayers in terms of criminal processing alone (not including the costs of long-term incarceration). The net dollar cost to taxpayers of this program is approximately $4,800 per child. The third column indicates the savings to taxpayers, including victim costs. Taking these saving into account, the early childhood education program saves the Washington State taxpayer almost $7,000 per child who attends the program. There are other intangible savings such as reduced use of social services, long-term employment resulting in greater tax revenue, etc. However, despite their clear benefits, these programs do not universally affect all children or their families to the same degree. Whereas the polio vaccine has all but eradicated polio in our country, it is unlikely that any primary prevention program, at least in the foreseeable future, will totally eradicate antisocial behavior. Unlike physical diseases, which typically have a single cause such as a virus, behavior has multiple causes; many of them are embedded in existing social systems which are out of the

Table 5.2. Examples of Cost Benefit of Selected Programs

Program	Cost/participant	Taxpayer benefits	Taxpayer and victim benefits combined
Nurse home visitation	$7,773	−$2,067	$15,918
Early childhood education	8,936	−4,754	6,972
Seattle Social Development Project	4,355	−456	14,169
Multisystemic therapy	4,743	31,661	131,918
Functional family therapy	2,161	14,149	59,067

Source: Adapted from S. Aos, P. Phipps, R. Bamoski, and R. Lieb (2001). *The comparative costs and benefits of programs to reduce crime (Ver. 4.0).* Olympia: Washington State Institute for Public Policy.

reach of psychological interventions. Antisocial behavior is, as the singing delinquents in *West Side Story* note, both a psychological and a "social disease." We know that there is a strong relationship between poverty and crime. A classic sociological study conducted some fifty years ago by Shaw and McKay in Chicago showed clearly that poorer neighborhoods had higher rates of delinquency as well as child abuse (Shaw and McKay, 1942). Thus, some of the ultimate risks associated with antisocial behavior in adolescence need to be addressed outside the realm of psychological or educational interventions.

Psychologist Uri Bronfenbrenner described the environment in which the individual lived as existing on multiple levels. The level on which the individual has the closest contact he referred to as the microsystem. Examples of microsystems include the family, school, and peer groups. The interactions of microsystems, such as a PTA group which brings parents and the school together, is referred to as a mesosystem. Most intervention (treatment or prevention) programs work on either the microsystem level, typically intervening with the family and/or the school in addition to directly intervening with the individual child or adolescent, for example parent management training. Others work with the mesosystem, two or more microsystems. An example of this is the Perry Pre School Program, which worked with children at their school as well as at their home. Another good example is multisystemic therapy (see chapter 4). Since risks exist at various environmental levels for these children—e.g., family, school, and peers—programs that address risk factors in different microsystems are more likely to succeed, as opposed to those that focus on just one area of the child's life.

Children who come from "normal" homes where they are loved and cared for and attend reasonably good schools where their special needs are met, and who have friends who don't engage in antisocial behavior, are much less likely to get into serious trouble during their adolescence. Prevention programs ultimately attempt to "normalize" the child's environment by providing parents with the necessary social supports and parenting skills, and/or helping the schools to provide the child with the proper social and cognitive skills. This is something most middle-class children are exposed to routinely. Universal, primary prevention programs try to provide children who are at risk, largely because they are poor, with an environment that approximates what children living in more affluent circumstances take for granted. Few prevention programs designed to reduce antisocial behavior target middle-class youth. This of course does not mean that middle-class children do not become delinquent. They do, and for many of the same reasons that poorer children do, but the occurrence of delinquency among middle-class children is lower because most of them have more social supports.

This brings us to the next level of the child's environment, which Bronfenbrenner referred to as the exosystem, which is the larger social context in which the child, his family, and school exist. It consists of employers, school boards, local governments, neighborhoods, etc. If the child's parents don't have opportunities for employment, this will impact negatively on the child; if the child's housing is substandard or the child lives in a high-density, high-crime neighborhood, this will have a negative impact.

Harold Leitenberg, a psychologist at the University of Vermont, addressed some of these issues in reviewing the impact of a number of prevention programs. He suggested that "[the] greatest impediment to successful delinquency prevention is the failure to address adequately the ultimate causes of delinquency" (Leitenberg, 1987, 320). He goes on to suggest that these causes are enmeshed in the political and social system and therefore are difficult to change. Leitenberg points out that the 1967 President's Commission on Law Enforcement and the Administration of Justice stated that issues such as housing, schools, and youth unemployment had to be addressed. These are issues that exist within the exosystem and cannot be altered by psychologists through treatment or prevention programs. Leitenberg concludes by stating that "unless the larger political, organizational, economic and social issues are addressed, I think we will make small headway, at best, in preventing delinquency" (329).

It is not that many of the programs I have discussed are not good. They are well designed and thoughtfully evaluated, but they may not be enough. Offering a mother-to-be help with her pregnancy and newborn is a great idea, but she and her child still have many years of struggle ahead of them after the intervention is over. For children living in poor, high-crime neighborhoods or other types of adverse circumstances it should not be unreasonable to think of providing them with additional services from infancy through adolescence. In the long run this would be less expensive than incarcerating them for part of their adolescent and adult years.

It is important to be aware of the fact that while the prevention programs which I have described were successful in many ways, the results, while not negligible, were not exceedingly strong either. Despite the fact that the percentage of adolescents arrested who attended the Perry Pre School program was significantly lower than those who did not, 31 percent of the individuals who attended the program, close to one in three, were arrested by the time they were young adults. This remains an exceedingly high and certainly unacceptable arrest rate for a population. Despite the many successes of the Seattle Social Development Program, the effects based on its own research were modest, and the program had less impact on the children at highest risk than on other children in the program. Yet it is unreasonable to expect even the best designed program to have a significant impact on all or even the large majority of the children who take part in it. There will be some who receive significant benefits, and others who benefit little. For the majority, it is possible to hope for some incremental gains that could, depending upon later interventions and life circumstances, lead to a relatively positive outcome.

The entire prevention process may need a conceptual change. Perhaps the focus shouldn't be on delinquency and violence, since ultimately the question really is how we can raise happy, healthy, and well-educated children even in the face of adverse circumstances. Clearly, while psychologists and other social scientists can do excellent work and provide excellent advice, they cannot be expected to do the job without the support of society at large. Despite the potential effectiveness of universal prevention programs such as Head Start, lead poisoning prevention, and Medicaid, psychologists Carol Ripple and Edward Zigler point out the United States as a nation rarely takes a preventive approach and tends to be more reactive than proactive. Furthermore they note that the United States is considerably behind other Western nations in providing comprehensive support for families (Ripple and Zigler, 2003). Given this national ethos it is unlikely that, despite the surgeon general and others who have called for a preventive approach to responding to the mental health needs of children, prevention programs will get the broad-based support that they deserve.

Conclusions

Prevention programs can be effective in reducing future behavior problems in young children. Even those programs that offer assistance to pregnant mothers and their newborns appear to be helpful. Providing support to primarily very young poor children and their families is a good thing to do, not only in terms of reducing or preventing conduct disorder but also in a moral sense. It seems unreasonable in a country as wealthy as ours to deprive any group of children of these basic opportunities and support systems, which after all are no more than those that are readily available to more affluent children.

On the other hand, these early interventions are not effective with all children. Children are embedded in various social systems, and unless significant changes are effected in those systems whatever gains the children may make are less likely to be sustained. Nonetheless, if the ongoing cycle of problematic parenting leading to problematic children leading to problematic adolescents leading once again to problematic parenting is to be broken, these prevention programs may be the best that we have to offer. It is unfortunate that despite their demonstrated positive impact on children's development and their cost effectiveness they are not more broadly applied across the country.

6
Summary and Conclusions

It's déjà vu all over again.
Yogi Berra

According to an article in the *New York Times* dated June 15, 2003, a sixteen-year-old California adolescent was sentenced to life in prison without the possibility of parole. The defendant was fourteen years old when, along with a twenty-nine-year-old accomplice, he kidnapped a businessman and shot at the police with an assault rifle during a chase. Fortunately, no one was injured. His lawyer pointed out that his client had only second-grade reading and math skills, that he had a traumatic family life, and had only a minor criminal history. There is no question that what this young man did was very bad. Kidnapping and attempted murder are very serious offenses. However, given the research that I have described, the California court's response to this young man's behavior seems less than enlightened. This is very much the essence of the problem. Research often does not influence policy. At least not in any direct way. So things do not change.

Defining delinquency is difficult because it is a social-legal term and as such will vary from one state and jurisdiction to another. So there is little consistency in conceptualizing who a delinquent is. For example, do three incidents of self-reported "minor" offenses (under $15) make an adolescent delinquent? Does one major assault constitute violent delinquent behavior? Epidemiologists Jane Costello and Adrian

Angold conclude: "The history of society's definition of, and response to, deviant children is more confused and contradictory than even this most difficult group of children should have to put up with. We still have not yet made up our minds how to respond to the basic issues of responsibility and culpability laid out by Plato 2500 years ago. Is it surprising that treatment has been so varied and, on the whole, so ineffective, given that we do not appear to have decided whose problem we are treating: the child's? the parents'? society's?" (Costello and Angold, 2001, 27). I suggested that it would be more consistent to think about juvenile delinquents as conduct-disordered adolescents. Conduct disorder, a psychiatric term, is a more reliable and universal definition. This would clarify who we are talking about and make the criteria for describing this group of adolescents more consistent.

It is difficult to determine the extent of delinquent behavior both in terms of incidence (how frequently the behavior occurs) and prevalence of the problem among the entire population of adolescents. The sources most often used to provide approximate answers to these questions are the Uniform Crime Reports, which record arrests, and self-report surveys, which ask the adolescent to report anonymously their antisocial behavior. However, neither of these is completely accurate. For instance, a study conducted by criminologists Dunford and Elliot (1984) found that 85 percent of individuals who self-reported serious delinquent behavior during adolescence *did not* have an official arrest record. Nonetheless, antisocial behavior in adolescents exists to a great enough degree to constitute a serious problem to society and to the children involved and warrants a great deal of attention. We can also conclude, based on the result of a number of studies, that a small percentage of adolescents, about 6 to 8 percent, are responsible for a large portion, about 60 percent, of the criminal behavior exhibited by adolescents.

We know that antisocial behavior in children and adolescents results from a combination of multiple risk factors which have been identified over and over again in a large number of studies. These include gender, socioeconomic status, family dynamics (including attachment, disciplinary practices, neglect, and abuse), ADHD, intellectual functioning, and neurological problems. In fact we know enough and have for some time known enough to be able to develop effective responses.

We are not clear about the role the adolescent developmental process plays in either generating or exacerbating antisocial behavior. For example, how do the changing biological, familial, psychological, and social factors impact on conduct disorder in adolescence? Nevertheless, numerous studies have shown that serious delinquent behavior begins in early adolescence and that it peaks in mid to late adolescence and then tapers off. We also know that the more serious delinquents typically begin behaving badly during the primary school years or earlier. In addition, research clearly indicates that antisocial peers play an important role in instigating and maintaining delinquency in adolescence but play a less important role during childhood. Researchers have also have recently discovered that the adolescent nervous system is not fully developed, in particular the frontal lobes, that part of the brain which is responsible for both planning and inhibition. This might account for the risk-taking behavior which is prevalent in adolescence as well as the antisocial behavior.

It would be reasonable to conclude that, though there is still some uncertainty, we have a fairly clear idea of why children become delinquent. What is also quite interesting is how we keep *re*discovering these factors. In reviewing the history of research and theory regarding delinquency over the past hundred years criminologist John Laub (2002) observed that the multiple causes which relate to delinquency (including individual, family, school, peer, and cultural factors) were first discussed in the early part of the twentieth century and then again reinvented or perhaps refined in the middle of the century and again at the end of century. For example, in their well-known book *Unraveling Juvenile Delinquency,* which was published in 1950, Sheldon and Eleanor Glueck reported the results of a large-scale study designed to differentiate delinquents from nondelinquents. They clearly identify the role of temperament, intellectual functioning, and the family as causal factors in delinquency as well as emphasizing the fact that delinquency is dependent on the interaction of all of these variables. Loeber and his colleagues (Loeber, Stouthamer-Loeber, Farrington, Lahey, Keenan, and White, 2002) list among the key findings of the Pittsburgh Youth

Study that "the higher the neighborhood disadvantage (as evident from the census data), the more likely boys are exposed to risk factors and the less likely that they will be exposed to promotive [protective] factors." This is a finding similar to Shaw and McKay (1942), who found that delinquency was concentrated in neighborhoods which had the greatest levels of infant mortality, low birth weight, and tuberculosis. In 1992, when laws requiring hospitals, doctors, and schools to report child abuse went into effect, psychologists James Garbarino and his colleague Kathleen Kostelny found that these same poor neighborhoods were also characterized by high rates of child abuse and neglect. How many times do we need to read that poor neighborhoods are bad for children and their families?

While there have been some new findings as a result of technology, particularly in the area of genetics and neurological functioning, many of the research findings of today are a repackaging or rediscovery of older findings, often without acknowledgment of the long history of the concept involved. Consider that the lyrics of the song used as the epigraph for this book were written in 1957. "Gee, Officer Krupke," sung by the gang members in the musical *West Side Story,* satirized the various psychological and social explanations for delinquent behavior half a century ago.

With regard to the juvenile justice system itself, I noted a significant number of studies and anecdotal materials which point to the fact that this system as it currently exists responds to the problems of young people who appear before it in an inconsistent and illogical manner. It is likely that it often does more harm than good, and it is in serious need of an overhaul. Some of this is the result of the fact that court calendars and intake personnel are so overloaded with cases that they cannot give the consideration necessary for adequate responses. Most of the family court judges I spoke with indicated that the system was overwhelmed and that intake workers had to handle double the load of cases that they could reasonably do well. One judge pointed out that that did not mean that the probation and intake workers were able to do an adequate job on half of their cases and only a fair job on the other half. Another judge indicated that as a result of the overloaded system adolescents had to be detained for a longer period of time before a hearing because it wasn't possible to get all the necessary information for the hearing together. In addition, adolescents are often detained before hearings unnecessarily, despite evidence that good alternatives to detention programs exist. Probation and aftercare services are often inadequate, increasing the likelihood that the youngster will engage in further antisocial behavior. It is not that there aren't good programs available; there are. But whether or not a youngster becomes involved in one of them is a "hit or miss" proposition, depending on the jurisdiction, availability of programs, monetary resources, etc. There are many good pilot projects around but no consistent, broadly applied approaches. Furthermore, even good programs may be cut. In Colorado a juvenile diversion project, designed to provide treatment to low-risk juvenile offenders as an alternate to traditional probation, was eliminated despite the fact that it was demonstrated to be both effective and cost efficient (Juvenile Justice Coalition, 2002).

There is a growing body of evidence that suggests that currently a number of treatment interventions result in positive outcomes for juvenile offenders. These include programs that focus on the youngster's psychosocial environment, such as functional family therapy, parent management training, and multisystemic therapy. Other programs that have proven to be effective provide adolescents with appropriate social and cognitive skills that they failed to develop earlier in their lives. The primary theoretical approaches that have proved to be useful have been behavior modification, cognitive/social learning theory, and systems theory.

Yet, there remains uncertainty regarding these treatments. While they can be successful with the majority of adolescents and/or their families, a substantial minority of youths who participate in these programs continue to commit crimes. Recall that for the over two hundred studies reviewed by Lipsey and Wilson, there was still an overall 44 percent recidivism rate for the youngsters who received treatment, although the outcomes were significantly better for specific interventions (Lipsey and Wilson, 1998). It is not clear why some adolescents or families respond to particular treatments and others do not. There is also the issue of the context in which the treatments occur. If, as most agree, the environment (including neighborhood, housing, schools, parental unemployment, etc.) plays a significant role in causing and maintaining juvenile delinquency, how effective can treatment programs be in the long run? It is similar to the dilemma that a public health model would have to address. For instance, while it is possible to treat a case of dysentery in a child, the problem is bound to reoccur if he or she continues to live in an environment where there is inadequate sanitation.

I noted that the surgeon general and others have recently emphasized the importance of early intervention, echoing the words of court psychiatrist William Healy (1915), who noted the potential benefits of beginning treatment early in the life of the child. Prevention is a two-part process; the first involves the accurate identification of young children who are likely to exhibit increasing levels of antisocial behavior as they age and the second involves developing programs designed to prevent this from happening. The studies I summarized demonstrate that it is indeed fairly easy to identify by at least age eight those children who are likely to become delinquent. This is because the best predictor of serious antisocial behavior in adolescence is serious antisocial behavior in childhood. Aggressive behavior tends to be fairly stable unless other factors intervene from childhood through adulthood. However, true primary prevention would have to intervene *prior to* the onset of notable age-inappropriate behavior and therefore begin quite early in life. Risk factors or predictors would have less to do with the behavior of the child than with the status of the mother or family. For example, young single mothers of low socioeconomic status are at greater risk of having offspring with behavior problems.

Current research seems to focus on further refinement of assessments to improve the accuracy with which they can predict later antisocial behavior. However, as I suggested earlier, this may be somewhat misguided, since it is equally important to identify children who will perform poorly in school or have substance abuse problems, or suffer from internalizing disorders such as depression or anxiety. It isn't clear why any potential problem(s) a child might have should not be identified early in his or her life and responded to in a meaningful way. In fact, there is a high degree of overlap between risk factors for academic-performance, mental-health, and substance-abuse problems and antisocial behavior. Furthermore, the emphasis on identifying and preventing conduct disorder shortchanges girls, who, coming from similar backgrounds as conduct-disordered boys, are more likely to suffer from internalizing disorders.

Prevention programs, as well as treatment programs, have met with some success. Universal programs that address the needs of expectant mothers throughout their pregnancy and through the early years of their child's life, such as the Elmira Nurse Home Visitation program, have proved beneficial and cost effective. These programs do not target antisocial behavior per se but rather focus on providing a better psychosocial environment for the child to grow in. That many, but not all, children benefit from such interventions and exhibit less antisocial behavior reinforces the idea that the problems that create antisocial behavior have their origins very early in life. Other universal, primary prevention programs, such as the Perry Pre School Program, target preschool children and their families, again prior to the onset of any signs of serious antisocial behavior. These programs have also resulted in reduced delinquent behavior in adolescence among the participants. Other important outcomes were that these children were more likely to complete high school, obtain some type of post–secondary school education and were more likely to be employed. Other programs I discussed included those which are applied in the primary grades. Some of these are applied to all children within the school, while others target those children who are already showing aggressive/antisocial behavior. Generally programs that involve both the child and his family have proved to be most useful.

While these programs have been helpful, it would be wrong to think that they are universally beneficial to all children. For example, children who participated in the Perry Pre School program did not differ significantly from the nonparticipants on a number of measures, including self-reported offenses, use of dangerous drugs, and the total number of convictions. These shortcomings are apparent in other prevention programs as well. There may be a number of reasons for this. First, many of these interventions are relatively short lived, lasting anywhere from two months to five years. Developmental theory would suggest that for programs to be truly effective they need to begin at infancy and continue through early adolescence, since there are significant risk factors that exist from birth onward through each stage of development. Children and their families need different types of support at each point along the child's developmental continuum. The needs of infants and toddlers are significantly different from those of eight year olds, and those of eight year olds are different from young adolescents. Gains made from early interventions need to be followed up and supported lest they be lost. This is particularly true for children and families who live in high-risk environments where housing is poor and crime and unemployment rates are high. For example, an unpublished longitudinal study followed inner-city children who had attended a pre-kindergarten program. As a result of attendance in the program their reading readiness scores were higher than children who had not attended. However, in the absence of any further support many of these children were reading *below* grade level by the time they were in the fourth grade (Hightower, 2003, personal communication).

In reviewing early intervention programs, psychologists Craig and Sharon Ramey (1998) of the University of Alabama suggest that the most effective early intervention programs are the ones that begin early in the child's life and continue for the longest period of time. They point out that effective programs are also more intensive, that is, they provide a high number of contact hours per week and per year. Furthermore, effective intervention programs are also comprehensive, providing educational, mental-health, physical-health, and social services. In other words, in addition to providing direct services to the child, they also create a more positive and supportive environment for the child during the entire time he or she is growing up. It is important to bear in mind that these solutions lie outside the juvenile justice system.

Delinquency and Politics

Some years ago I was giving a lecture on child abuse to an interdisciplinary class. Since it was a team-taught class, professors of history, English, and sociology were also present. When I was finished discussing the psychological impact of child abuse, the sociology professor said that child abuse was ultimately a political issue. While I did not contradict her, I thought to myself, "There goes that leftist radical spouting off about politics again." Now I think she was making a very important point. In the foreword to the recent text *A Century of Juvenile Justice,* Adele Simmons, past president of the MacArthur Foundation, asks the following question:

> What is distressing is the extent to which all that we know about prevention and intervention does not shape public policy. If we do not want to spend more money on jails and prisons, why do we not invest more in early childhood education and after school programs? Why do we insist on imprisoning children with adults when we know that policy almost insures that the child will be imprisoned again and again as an adult? How can we explain why states fail to make investments that will help young offenders become effective members of their community? (Simmons, 2002, x, xi)

She is quite right to ask these questions. Research over the past decades has significantly improved our understanding of the development of delinquency, leading to the development and evaluation of improved prevention and intervention techniques. Research has also identified problems within a seriously overburdened juvenile justice system. However, it is not reasonable to assume that further research *alone* will have any significant impact on the scope of the problem of juvenile delinquency. Clearly it has not in the past, and it will not now. The research keeps academics busy and the grant money flowing in, but in truth the big picture hasn't changed all that much over the past hundred years. While the rates of juvenile delinquency have declined over the past ten years, no one has suggested that this is the result of our greater understanding of the problem or our improved intervention techniques. This lack of progress is actually quite remarkable. By way of comparison, consider the progress that has been made in the field of aviation since the Wright Brothers made their first flight about one hundred years ago.

Why is this true? I think it is because researchers publish largely for an academic audience. Relevant information doesn't always get, at least not directly, to the people who are in a position to implement law and policies that would have an effect. And if it does, they are frequently not inclined to do very much about it. As part of my research for this book, I felt it would be worthwhile to meet with a number of my New York State legislators. I asked them whether research which demonstrated that prevention would, over the long run, be a more effective way of dealing with the problem of delinquency, had any impact on their legislative agenda. The answer they gave me was that their constituents were concerned with immediate results and that it would be very difficult to get *reelected* on the basis of making long-term promises that *might* eventually pay off. Allocating money for building prisons and juvenile detention facilities and putting more police on the streets demonstrates a more immediate response, contains the existing problem, provides jobs, and is thus a more politically expedient gesture. The former commissioner of juvenile justice for a large state in the Northeast told me that he resigned from his job because he was unable to convince the state legislators that there was an advantage to depopulating overcrowded juvenile institutions and improving reentry and probation services. State legislators, he said, wanted to spend their money on more "law and order."

Legislators typically respond to political pressure, in terms of votes and campaign donations. Unions, industries, and special interest groups such as the NRA typically have political clout because they can deliver votes, money, or—better still—both. Most children who are "at risk" for future behavior problems are poor, and disproportionate numbers of them are minorities. They can deliver neither money nor votes, so they don't wind up very high on the "to do" list on the legislative agenda. In essence they are disenfranchised. An African American state legislator from a city in upstate New York said to me: "There's not much I can do. I'd just be another black face asking for money for poor people."

My colleague from the sociology department was in fact correct; it is about politics. Yale psychologists Edward Zigler and Carol Ripple (2003) have the following to say on the federal government's failure to take an effective role in prevention programs: "The answer lies in *politics*—implementing policy-driven prevention is at heart a political process—and in the programs' underlying ideological limitations. . . . By targeting marginalized, typically low-income families, the policies allow policymakers (the 'haves') to distance themselves from the program recipients (the 'have nots'). Programs that are formulated to serve only low-income groups, then, are subject to political sidelining" (Ripple and Zigler, 2003, 487 [italics added]).

Zigler and Ripple are not the only ones to identify political issues as the heart of the matter. Psychologists Craig and Sharon Ramey (see above), after discussing early interventions for vulnerable children, conclude: "The *primary* issues for early intervention now are ones of the *political* will to aid vulnerable children, [and] the appropriate scale of resources needed to provide potentially effective interventions" (Ramey and Ramey, 1998, 119 [italics added]). Similarly Harold Leitenberg of the University of Vermont, after reviewing a number of primary prevention programs, concluded: "I think the most productive area for delinquency prevention is not within the realm of psychology, sociology, psychiatry, social work or criminology—it is within the area of *politics* (Leitenberg, 1987, 329 [italics added]). The policy recommendations which typically appear at the end of articles or books on antisocial adolescents do not mean very much if they are not going to be implemented.

What legislators did say was effective, at least in terms of getting information to them, were advocacy groups, (which essentially are lobbying groups) which could bring issues and research that related to delinquency to the attention of state legislators. I attended several meetings of one such organization, the New York Juvenile Justice Coalition, as they prepared for a meeting with state legislators to advocate for reduced use of pretrial detention, improved post-release service, better community programs for youth who had been in difficulty with the law, and youth employment programs. I went with them to Albany when they met with the legislators from both the New York State Senate and Assembly. After breaking up into teams of five or six people, which included the young people who would directly benefit from these proposals, we went to the offices of four state legislators. (Each team visited different legislators so that these issues were raised with a significant number of legislators in the Senate and Assembly by the end of the day.) In the meetings I attended the legislators (or sometimes their aides) listened politely and appeared interested in the issues that were raised. It remains to be seen what will ultimately be accomplished.

Perhaps in addition to funding further research, money should also be spent on determining more effective ways of providing policy-makers with relevant information and proposing and supporting meaningful legislation that would result in improved neighborhoods and schools and that would support statewide programs to provide the necessary psychological and educational support to children and families at risk throughout childhood and adolescence. This may seem like a very tall order, but it is doable if it can be supported by both the federal and state governments. For example, there have been a number of successful prevention programs such as the Elmira home visitation program, the Perry Pre School Project, the FAST Track program, the Seattle Social Development Program, and others. Programs such as these should move from being programs which are irregularly implemented to being administered on a statewide basis, though this would not preclude further evaluations and refinement of these programs.

Attending to the implementation of what we already know is effective should take precedence over research. Otherwise, we will continue to preach to the choir and no converts will be won. I recently had a conversation with a state legislator, Assemblyman Joseph Errigo, who was interested in following up on some of the questions I raised regarding the interface between legislation and social science research. Assemblyman Errigo is from upstate New York and is the ranking minority member of the committee for children and families, an important committee that introduces legislation relevant to many of the issues that I have raised in this book. He introduced me to a legislative colleague, Assemblyman David Gantt from Rochester, and I summarized some of the research on delinquency prevention programs for him; after we talked for a while he said to me, "You know, Joe, and I never talked about this before. You've been sort of a catalyst." Assemblyman Errigo asked if I could provide him with a cost benefit analysis of primary prevention programs (which I did). He suggested that he would like to form a coalition of area legislators to institute a public education program on the benefits and advantages of early intervention. I found their response interesting, since I was meeting with them to collect information, not to serve as an advocate. I don't know whether anything will come of this brief discussion; however, meeting and providing legislators with relevant research may be one of the more important functions that social scientists can carry out at this time.

There are some good models to follow. The state of Washington created a Washington State Institute for Public Policy. This institute, which is staffed by policy analysts, academic specialists, and consultants, works closely with state legislators and provides them with evaluations and cost benefit analyses of effective prevention and intervention programs, which are then funded by the legislature and applied on a statewide basis (Aos, Phillips, Bamoski, and Lieb, 2001). At the very least this is a more effective way of utilizing relevant research and can have a real impact on the problem of delinquency in terms of judicial policy, treatment, and prevention. Clearly, research findings and policy recommendations are of no value unless they are implemented in a consistent and logical way, without undue influence of political considerations.

The problem of delinquency is a reflection of our society's indifference to the lives of largely poor children and our need to control rather than understand the problem. This is not a liberal political position (which it certainly sounds like) but rather reflects the findings of current and past research. Delinquency and other difficulties affecting children and adolescents will not cease to be a significant problem until we as a nation respond to the needs of these young people with adequate attention and resources. To date there is no momentum toward that aim.

Further Reading

The following are some excellent recent sources on juvenile delinquency.

Hill, J., and Maughn, B. (eds.). (2001). *Conduct disorders in childhood and adolescence.* Cambridge, UK: Cambridge University Press.

Loeber, R., and Farrington, D. P. (eds.). (1998). *Serious and violent juvenile offenders: Risk factors and successful interventions.* Thousand Oaks, CA: Sage.

McCord, J., Spatz-Windom, C., Crowell, N. (eds.). (2001). *Juvenile crime, juvenile justice.* Washington, DC: National Academy Press.

Rosenheim, M., Zimirig, F., Tananhaus, D., and Dohrn, B. (eds.). (2002). *A Century of juvenile justice.* Chicago, IL: University of Chicago Press.

The web site of the Office of Juvenile Justice and Delinquency Prevention is particularly helpful: www.ojjdp.ncjrs.org. It also contains links and references to other relevant sources and web sites.

References

Aber, J. L., Brown, J. L., and Jones, S. M. (2003). Developmental trajectories toward violence in middle childhood: Course, demographic differences, and response to school-based intervention. *Developmental Psychology*, 39, 324–348.

Aichhorn, A. (1935). *Wayward youth*. New York: Viking Press.

Alexander, J. F., and Parsons, B. V. (1982). *Functional family therapy*. Monterey, CA: Brooks/Cole.

Allen, J. P., Marsh, P., McFarland, C., McElhaney, K. P., Land, D. J., Jodl, K. M., and Peck, S. (2002). Attachment and autonomy as predictors of the development of social skills and delinquency during midadolescence. *Journal of Consulting and Clinical Psychology*, 70, 56–66.

American Psychiatric Association. (1994). *Diagnostic and statistical manual* (4th ed.). Washington, DC: Author.

Anderson, C. A., Berkowitz, L., Donnerstein, E., Huesman, L. R., Johnson, J., Linz, D., Malmuth, N., and Wartella, E. (2003). The influence of media violence on youth. *Psychological Science in the Public Interest*, 4, 81–110.

Aos, S., Phipps, P., Bamoski, R., and Lieb, R. (2001). The comparative costs and benefits of programs to reduce crime (Ver. 4.0). Olympia, WA: Washington State Institute for Public Policy.

Arnett, J. J. (1999). Adolescent storm and stress reconsidered. *American Psychologist*, 54, 317–326.

Associated Press. (2003, June 15). California teenager given life sentence. *New York Times*, p. 21.

Bandura, A., and Walters, R. H. (1963). *Social learning and personality development*. New York: Holt, Rinehart, and Winston.

Beck, A. T. (1976). *Cognitive therapy and the emotional disorders*. New York: International Universities Press.

Bernstein, L., and Sondheim, S. (1957). "Gee, Officer Krupke." From *West Side Story*. New York: Columbia Broadway Masterworks.

Berruta-Clement, J. R., Schweinhart, L. J., Barnett, W. S., and Weikart, D. P. (1987). The effects of early educational intervention on crime and delinquency in adolescence and early adulthood. In J. D. Burchard and S. N. Burchard (eds.), *Prevention of delinquent behavior*. Newbury Park, CA: Sage.

Blos, P. (1962). *On Adolescence: A psychoanalytic interpretation*. New York: Free Press.

Bowlby, J. (1969). *Attachment and loss: Volume I. Attachment*. New York: Basic Books.

Brandt, D. (1979). Development of intake criteria in a day treatment program for delinquent boys. *Psychological Reports,* 44, 1028–1030.

Bronfenbrenner, U. (1979). *The Ecology of human development: Experiments by nature and design.* Cambridge, MA: Harvard University Press.

Brooks, J. H., and Reddon, J. R. (1996). Serum testosterone levels in violent and non violent young offenders. *Journal of Clinical Psychology,* 52, 475–483.

Buchanan, C. M., Eccles, J. S., and Becker, J. B. (1992). Are adolescents the victims of raging hormones: Evidence for *activational* effects of hormones on moods and behavior at adolescence. *Psychological Bulletin,* 111, 62–107.

Carr, M., and Vandiver, T. (2001). Risk and protective factors among youth offenders. *Adolescence,* 36, 409–427.

Caspi, A., McClay, J., Moffit, T. E., Mill, J., Martin, J., Craig, I. W., Taylor, A., and Poulton, R. (2002). Role of genotype in the cycle of violence in maltreated children. *Science,* 297, 851–854.

Chamberlain, P., and Reid, J. B. (1998). Comparison of two community alternatives to incarceration for chronic juvenile offenders. *Journal of Consulting and Clinical Psychology,* 66, 624–633.

Community defense clinic at New York University School of Law. (2001). Parole or remand: A study of the hidden factors affecting juvenile detention in New York City.

Conduct Problems Prevention Research Group. (1999). Initial impact of the Fast Track Prevention Program: I. The high-risk sample. *Journal of Consulting and Clinical Psychology,* 67, 631–647.

Costello, E. J., and Angold, A. (2001). Bad behaviour: An historical perspective on disorders of conduct. In J. Hill and B. Maughan (eds.), *Conduct disorders in childhood and adolescence* (pp. 1–31). Cambridge, UK: Cambridge University Press.

Costello, E. J., Compton, S. K., Keeler, G., and Angold, A. (2003). Relationship between poverty and psychopathology: A natural experiment. *Journal of the American Medical Association,* 290, 2023–2029.

Davey, M., and Wilgren, J. (2005, March 24). *New York Times,* pp. A1 and A14.

Dishion, T., McCord, J., and Poulin, F. (1999). When interventions harm: Peer groups and problem behavior. *American Psychologist,* 54, 755–764.

Dodge, K. A. (1991). The structure and function of reactive and proactive aggression. In D. J. Pepler and K. H. Rubin (eds.), *The development and treatment of childhood aggression.* Hillsdale, NJ: Lawrence Erlbaum Associates.

Dodge, K. A., Pettit, G. S., and Bates, J. E. (1997). How the experience of early physical abuse leads children to become chronically aggressive. *Developmental perspectives on trauma: Theory research and intervention,* 8, 263–288.

Dunford, F. W., and Elliot, D. S. (1984). Identifying career offenders using self-report data. *Journal of Research in Crime and Delinquency,* 21, 57–86.

Eisler, K. R. (ed.). (1949). *Searchlights on delinquency*. New York: International Universities Press.

Eley, T. (1997). General genes: A new theme in developmental psychopathology. *Current Directions in Psychological Science, 6,* 90–95.

Elliot, D. S., and Menard, S. (1996). Delinquent friends and delinquent behavior. In J. D. Hawkins (ed.), *Delinquency and crime: Current theories.* Cambridge, UK: Cambridge University Press.

Erikson, E. (1957). The confirmation of the delinquent. *Chicago Review,* 10, 15–23.

———. (1968). *Identity: Youth and crisis.* New York: Norton.

Erikson, M. F., Sroufe, A. L., and Egeland, B. (1985). The relationship between quality of attachment and behavior problems in preschool in a high risk sample. In I. Bretherton and E. Waters (eds.), *Growing points of attachment: Theory and research.* Chicago, IL: Monographs of the Society for Research in Child Development, University of Chicago Press.

Evans, G. W. (2004). The environment of childhood poverty. *American Psychologist, 59,* 77–92.

Fagan, J. (1995). Separating the men from the boys: The comparative advantage of juvenile versus criminal court sanctions on recidivism among adolescent felony offenders. In J. C. Howell, B. Krisberg, J. D. Hawkins, and J. J. Wilson (eds.), *A sourcebook: Serious, violent and chronic juvenile offenders.* Thousand Oaks, CA: Sage.

Farrington, D. P. (1996). The explanation and prevention of youthful offending. In J. D. Hawkins (ed.), *Delinquency and crime: Current theories.* Cambridge, UK: Cambridge University Press.

Farrington, D. P., and Loeber, R. (1999). Transatlantic replicability of risk factors in the development of delinquency. In P. Cohen, C. Slomkowski, and L. N. Robbins (eds.), *Historical and geographical influences on psychopathology.* Mahwah, NJ: Lawrence Erlbaum Associates.

Faruquee, M. (2002). *Rethinking juvenile detention in New York City: A report by the Juvenile Justice Project of the Correctional Association of New York.* Unpublished manuscript.

Federal Bureau of Investigation. *Crime in the United States.* Washington, DC: U.S. Department of Justice.

Federal Bureau of Investigation, National Center for the Analysis of Violent Crime. (2000). *The school shooter: A threat assessment perspective.* Retrieved from www.fbi.gov.

Finger, J., and Silverman, M. (1966). Changes in academic performance in the junior high school. *Personnel and Guidance Journal, 45,* 157–164.

Fisher, P. A., and Chamberlain, P. (2000). Multidimensional treatment foster care: A program for intensive parenting, family support, and skill building. *Journal of Emotional and Behavior Disorders, 8,* 155–165.

Flannery, D. J. (2003). Initial behavior outcomes for the Peace Builders universal school-based violence prevention program. *Developmental Psychology*, 39, 292–308.

Freud, A. (1958). *Psychoanalytic study of the child*. 13, 255–278. New York: International Universities Press.

Friedlander, K. (1949). Delinquency and ego development. In K. R. Eissler (ed.), *Searchlights on delinquency*. New York: International Universities Press.

Garbarino, J., and Kostelny, K. (1992). Child maltreatment as a community problem. *International Journal of Child Abuse and Neglect*, 16, 455–464.

Garrett, C. (1985). Effects of residential treatment on adjudicated delinquents: A meta-analysis. *Journal of Research in Crime and Delinquency*, 22, 287–308.

Geurra, N., Huesmann, L. R., and Spindler, A. (2003). Community violence exposure, social cognition and aggression among urban elementary school children. *Child Development*, 74, 1561–1576.

Giancola, S. P. (2000). Adolescent behavior problems: Peer pressure *is* all it is cracked up to be. *ERIC/CASS virtual library*. Retrieved from www.ericcass.uncg.edu/virtuallib/violence/9008.html.

Gjone, H., and Stevenson, J. (1997). A longitudinal twin study of temperament and behavior problems: Common genetic or environmental influences? *Journal of the American Academy of Child and Adolescent Psychiatry*, 36, 1448–1456.

Glueck, S., and Glueck, E. (1950). *Unraveling juvenile delinquency*. Cambridge, MA: Harvard University Press.

Gorenstien, E. E. (1990). Neuropsychology of juvenile delinquency. *Forensic Reports*, 3, 15–48.

Gottesman, I., Goldsmith, H., and Carey, G. (1997). A developmental and a genetic perspective on aggression. In *Uniting psychology and biology: Integrative perspectives on human development*. Washington, DC: American Psychological Association.

Greenhouse, L. (2004, January 27). Supreme Court to review using execution in juvenile cases. *New York Times*, p. A1.

Grisso, T., and Schwartz, R. (eds.). (2000). *Youth on trial: A developmental perspective on juvenile justice*. Chicago, IL: University of Chicago Press.

Hall, G. S. (1905). *Adolescence*. New York: D. Appleton.

Hartman, H. (1958). *Ego psychology and the problem of adaptation*. New York: International Universities Press.

Hawkins, J. D., Catalano, R. F., Kosterman, R., Abbot, R., and Hill, K. G. (1999). Preventing adolescent health-risk behaviors by strengthening protection during childhood. *Archives of Pediatrics and Adolescent Medicine*, 153, 226–234.

Hawkins, J. D., Herrenkohl, T., Farrington, D. P., Brewer, D., Catalano, R. F., and Harachi, T. W. (1998). In R. Loeber and D. P. Farrington (eds.), *Seri-*

ous and violent juvenile offenders (pp. 106–146). Thousand Oaks, CA: Sage.

Healy, W. (1915). *The Individual Delinquent.* Boston, MA: Little, Brown.

———. (1917). *Mental Conflicts and Misconduct.* Boston, MA: Little, Brown.

Healy, W., and Bronner, A. (1926). *Delinquents and criminals: Their making and unmaking.* New York: Macmillan.

Henggeler, S. W., Melton, G. B., and Smith, L. A. (1992). Family preservation using multisystemic therapy: An effective alternative to incarcerating serious juvenile offenders. *Journal of Consulting and Clinical Psychology,* 60, 953–961.

Henggeler, S. W., Schoenwald, S. K., Borduin, C. M., Rowlands, M. D., and Cunningham, P. B. (1998). *Multisystemic treatment of antisocial behavior in children and adolescents.* New York: Guilford Press.

Hightower, D. (2003, June 10). Personal Communication.

Huey, Jr., S. J., Henggeler, S. W., Brondino, M. J., and Pickrel, S. G. (2000). Mechanisms of change in Multisytemic Therapy: Reducing delinquent behavior through therapist adherence and improved family and peer functioning. *Journal of Consulting and Clinical Psychology,* 68, 451–467.

Johnson, M. B. (2001). *NJ Advisor* 6, 14–18.

Juvenile Justice Coalition. (2002) Unpublished study. Washington, DC: Author.

Kazdin, A. (1996). *Conduct disorders in childhood and adolescence* (2nd ed.). Thousand Oaks, CA: Sage.

Kazdin, A. (2001). Treatment of conduct disorders. In J. Hill and B. Maughan (eds.), *Conduct disorders in childhood and adolescence.* Cambridge, UK: Cambridge University Press.

Kazdin, A., and Kagan, J. (1994). Models of dysfunction in developmental psychopathology. *Clinical Psychology: Science and Practice,* 16, 320–328.

Kazdin, A., Siegel, T. C., and Bass, D. (1992). Cognitive problem-solving skills training and parent management training in the treatment of antisocial behavior in children. *Journal of Consulting and Clinical Psychology,* 60, 733–747.

Kokko, K., and Pulkkinen, L. (2000). Aggression in childhood and long-term unemployment in adulthood: A cycle of maladaption and some protective factors. *Developmental Psychology,* 36, 463–472.

Kolata, G. (2002, March 30). A study finds more links between tv and violence. *New York Times,* p. A25.

Krisberg, B., and Howell, J. (1998). Impact of the juvenile justice system and prospects for graduated sanctions. In R. Loeber and D. P. Farrington (eds.), *Serious and violent juvenile offenders: Risk factors and successful interventions.* Thousand Oaks, CA: Sage.

Lally, J. R., Mangione, P. L., and Honig, A. S. (1988). The Syracuse University Family Development Research Program: Long-range impact of an early

intervention with low income children and their families. In D. R. Pow-
ell (ed.), *Advances in applied developmental psychology: Parent education as
early childhood intervention: Emerging directions in theory, research and
practice* (pp. 79–104). Norwood, NJ: Ablex.

Laub, J. H. (2002). A century of delinquency research and delinquency theory. In
M. Rosenheim, F. Zimring, D. Tanenhaus, and B. Dohrn (eds.), *A century
of juvenile justice,* pp. 179–205. Chicago, IL: University of Chicago Press.

Leitenberg, H. (1987). Primary prevention of delinquency. In J. D. Burchard
and S. N. Burchard (eds.), *Prevention of delinquent behavior* (pp. 312–
330). Newbury Park, CA: Sage.

Lewis, D., Pincus, J. H., Lovely, R., Spitzer, E., and Moy, E. (1987). Biopsy-
chosocial characteristics of matched samples of delinquents and nondelinquents. *Journal of the American Academy of Child and Adolescent Psychiatry,* 26, 744–752.

Lipsey, M. W., and Derzon, J. H. (1998). Predictors of violent or serious delinquency in adolescence and early adulthood. In R. Loeber and D. P. Farrington (eds.), *Serious and violent juvenile offenders* (pp. 86–105). Thousand Oaks, CA: Sage.

Lipsey, M. W., and Wilson, D. B. (1998). Effective intervention for serious juvenile offenders: A synthesis of research. In R. Loeber and D. P. Farrington
(eds.), *Serious and violent juvenile offenders* (pp. 313–345). Thousand
Oaks, CA: Sage.

Loeber, R., and Dishion, T. J. (1983). Early predictors of male delinquency: A
review. *Psychological Bulletin,* 94, 68–99.

Loeber, R., and Farrington, D. P. (2000). Young children who commit crime:
Epidemiology, developmental origins, risk factors, early interventions
and policy implications. *Development and Psychopathology,* 12, 737–762.

Loeber, R., Farrington, D. P., Stouhamer-Loeber, M., and Van Kammen, W. B.
(1998). *Antisocial behavior and mental health problems: Explanatory factors
in childhood and adolescence.* Mahwah, NJ: Lawrence Erlbaum Associates.

Loeber, R., Stouthamer-Loeber, M., Farrington, D. P., Lahey, B. B., Keenan, K.,
and White, H. R. (2002). Editorial introduction: Three longitudinal
studies of children's development in Pittsburgh: The Developmental
Trends Study, the Pittsburgh Youth Study, and the Pittsburgh Girls Study.
Criminal Behavior and Mental Health, 12, 1–23.

Lombroso-Ferrero, G. (1972). *Criminal man.* Montclair, NJ: Patterson Mith.
Originally published in 1911.

Lynman, D. R., and Henry, B. (2001). The role of neuropsychological deficits in
conduct disorders. In J. Hill and B. Maughan (eds.), *Conduct disorder in
childhood and adolescence* (pp. 235–263). Cambridge, UK: Cambridge
University Press.

MacArthur Foundation. Retrieved on April 23, 2004, from www.mac-adoldev-
juvjustice.org.

Maugan, B., and Rutter, M. (2001). Antisocial children grow up. In J. Hill and B. Vaughan (eds.), *Conduct disorders in childhood and adolescence.* Cambridge, UK: Cambridge University Press.

McCord, J., Tremblay, R E., Vitaro, F., and Desmarais-Gervais, L. (1994). Boys' disruptive behavior, school adjustment and delinquency: The Montreal prevention experiment. *International Journal of Behavioral Development,* 17, 739–752.

McCord, J., Spatz-Windom, C., Crowell, N. (eds.). (2001). *Juvenile crime, juvenile justice.* Washington, DC: National Academy Press.

McLoyd, V. C. (1998). Socioeconomic disadvantage and child development. *American Psychologist,* 53, 185–204.

McManus, M., Alessi, N. E., Grapentine, W. L., and Brickman, A. (1984). Psychiatric disturbance in serious delinquents. *Journal of the American Academy of Child Psychiatry,* 23, 602–615.

Mead, M. (1950). *Coming of age in Samoa.* New York: New American Library (originally published in 1928).

Mednick, S. A., Gabrielli, W. F., and Hutchings, B. (1984). Genetic influences in criminal convictions: Evidence from an adoption cohort. *Science,* 22, 891–894.

Moffit, T. E. (1993). Adolescence-limited and life-course-persistent antisocial behavior: A developmetal taxonomy. *Psychological Review,* 100, 674–701.

Moffit, T. E., and Caspi, A. (2001). Childhood predictors differentiate life-course persistent and adolescence-limited antisocial pathways among males and females. *Development and Psychopathology,* 13, 355–375.

National Crime Victimization Survey. (1995). Washington, DC: Bureau of Justice Statistics.

National Institute of Mental Health. (1982). *Television and behavior: Ten years of scientific progress and implications for the eighties, Summary Report* (Vol. 1). Washington, DC: U.S. Government Printing Office.

National Research Council. (1993). *Losing generations: Adolescents in high risk settings.* Washington, DC: National Academy Press.

O'Donnel, J., Hawkins, J. D., Catalano, R. F., Abbot, R. D., and Day, L. E. (1995). Preventing school failure, drug use, and delinquency among low income children: Long term intervention in elementary schools. *American Journal of Orthopsychiatry,* 65, 87–100.

Office of Juvenile Justice and Delinquency Prevention. (1999). National Longitudinal Survey of Youth. Cited in *Juvenile offenders and victims: 1999 National report.* Washington, DC: Author.

———. (2001). *Blueprints for violence prevention.* Washington, DC: Author.

Olds, D. L., Eckenrode, J., and Henderson, C. R., Jr. (1997). Long-term effects of home visitation on maternal life course and child abuse and neglect. *Journal of the American Medical Association,* 278, 637–643.

Olds, D. L., Henderson, C. R., Jr., and Cole, R. (1998). Long-term effects of nurse home visitation on children's criminal and antisocial behavior: 15 year follow up of a randomized controlled trial. *Journal of the American Medical Association,* 280, 1238–1244.

Olweus, D. (1979). Stability of aggressive reaction patterns in males: A review. *Psychological Bulletin,* 86, 852–875.

Parent, D. G., Lieter, V., Kennedy, S., Livens, L., Wentworth, D., and Wilcox, S. (1994). *Condition of confinement: Juvenile detention and corrections facilities.* Washington, DC: U.S. Department of Justice, Office of Juvenile Justice and Delinquency Prevention.

Patterson, G. R., Capaldi, D., and Bank, L. (1991). An early starter model for predicting delinquency. In D. J. Pepler and K. H. Rubin (eds.), *The development and treatment of childhood aggression* (pp. 139–168). Hillsdale, NJ: Lawrence Erlbaum Associates.

Pollak, S. D., and Tolley-Schell, S. A. (2003) Selective attention to facial emotion in physically abused children. *Journal of Abnormal Psychology,* 112, 323–338.

Ramey, C. T., and Ramey, S. L. (1998). Early intervention and early experience. *American Psychologist,* 53, 109–120.

Redlich, A. D., Silverman, M., and Steiner, H. (2003). Pre-adjudicative and adjudicative competence in juveniles and young adults. *Behavioral Sciences and the Law,* 21, 393–410.

Ripple, C. H., and Zigler, E. (2003). Research, policy and the federal role in prevention initiatives for children. *American Psychologist,* 58,482–490.

Robbins, L. (1978). Sturdy childhood predictors of antisocial behavior: replications from longitudinal studies. *Psychological Medicine,* 8, 611–622.

Roper v. Simmons 1255.ct 1183, 2005 Lexis 2200 (2005).

Rosenheim, M. K. (2002). The modern American juvenile court. In M. K. Rosenheim, F. E. Zimring, D. S. Tanahaus, and B. Dohrn (eds.), *A century of juvenile justice.* Chicago, IL: University of Chicago Press.

Rothstien, R. (2002, June 5). Lessons. *New York Times,* p. B8.

Satcher, D. (2001). *Youth violence: A report from the surgeon general.* Washington, DC: U.S. Public Health Service.

Schwartz, C. E., Snidman, N., and Kagan, J. (1996). Early childhood temperament as a determinant of externalizing behavior in adolescence. *Development and Psychopathology,* 8, 527–537.

Seitz, V., Rosenbaum, L. K., and Apfel, N. H. (1985). Effects of family support intervention: A ten year follow up. *Child Development,* 56, 376–391.

Shaw, C., and McKay, H. (1942). *Juvenile delinquency and urban areas.* Chicago, IL: University of Chicago Press.

Simmons, A. (2002). Foreword. In M. K. Rosenheim, F. E. Zimring, D. S. Tanenhaus, and B. Dohrn (eds.), *A century of juvenile justice* (pp. ix–xi). Chicago, IL: University of Chicago Press.

Snyder, H. N. (2003). *Juvenile arrests 2001.* Washington DC: Office of Juvenile Justice and Delinquency Prevention.

Snyder, H. N., and Sickmund, M. (1999). *Juvenile offenders and victims: 1999 National report.* Washington, DC: Office of Juvenile Justice and Delinquency Prevention.

Steinberg, L., and Scott, E. S. (2003). Less guilty by reason of adolescence: Developmental immaturity, diminished responsibility and the juvenile death penalty. *American Psychologist,* 58, 1009–1018.

Talbot, M. (2000, September 10). The maximum security adolescent. *New York Times Magazine,* 40–96.

Teichner, G., and Golden, C. J. (2000). The relationship of neuropsychological impairment to conduct disorder in adolescence: A conceptual review. *Aggressions and Violent Behavior,* 5, 509–528.

Thornberry, T. P. (1998). Membership in youth gangs and involvement in serious and violent offending. In R. Loeber and D. P. Farrington (eds.), *Serious and violent juvenile offenders.* Thousand Oaks, CA: Sage.

Tracy, P., Wolfgang, M., and Figlio, R. (1985). U.S. Department of Justice, Office of Juvenile Justice and Delinquency Prevention.

United States Bureau of the Census, Current Population Reports. (1997). *Poverty in the United States: Consumer income.* (Series P60–201). Washington, DC: U.S. Government Printing Office.

United States Bureau of Justice Statistics. (1995), *National Crime Victimization Survey* (202/6333047). Washington, DC: U.S. Government Printing Office.

United States Department of Justice. (1999). *Juvenile offenders and victims: 1999 national report.* Washington, DC: Author.

Von Zielbauer, P. (2004, January 16). Rikers houses low-level inmates at high expenses. *New York Times,* p. 1.

———. (2005, March 1). *New York Times,* pp. A1 and A20.

Wasserman, G., Miller, L., Pinner, E., and Jaramillo, B. S. (1996). Parenting predictors of conduct problems in high risk boys. *Journal of the American Academy of Child and Adolescent Psychiatry,* 35, 1227–1236.

Webster-Stratton, C., and Reid, M. J. (2003). Treating conduct problems and strengthening social and emotional competence in young children: The Dina Dinosaur Treatment Program. *Journal of Emotional and Behavioral Disorders,* 11, 130–143.

Webster-Stratton, C., Reid, M. J., and Hammond, M. (2001). Preventing conduct problems, promoting social competence: A parent and teacher training partnership in Head Start. *Journal of Clinical Child Psychology,* 30, 283–302.

Werner, E. E. (1987). Vulnerability and resiliency in children at risk for delinquency: A longitudinal study from birth to adulthood. In J. D. Burchard and S. N. Burchard (eds.), *Prevention of delinquent behavior* (pp. 16–43). Newbury Park, CA: Sage.

Wilson, J. Q. (1998). Never too early. In R. Loeber and D. P. Farrington (eds.), *Serious and violent juvenile offenders.* Thousand Oaks, CA: Sage.

Wilson, J. Q., and Herrnstein, R. J. (1985). *Crime and human nature*. New York: Simon and Schuster.

Windle, M. (2000). A latent growth curve model of delinquent activity among adolescents. *Applied Developmental Science,* 4, 193–208.

Winnicott, D. W. (1960). The theory of the parent-infant relationship. *International Journal of Psychoanalysis,* 41, 585–595.

Zigler, E., Taussig, C., and Black, K. (1992). Early childhood intervention: A promising preventative for juvenile delinquency. *American Psychologist,* 47, 997–1006.

Zoccolillo, M. (1992). Co-occurrence of conduct disorders and its adult outcomes with depressive and anxiety disorders: A review. *Journal of the American Academy of Child and Adolescent Psychiatry,* 30, 973–981.

———. (1993). Gender and the development of conduct disorder. *Development and Psychopathology,* 5, 65–78.

Index

Abuse, 14–15, 63, 64, 65, 127, 134, 138–139
ADHD, 1, 6, 18, 34, 60–62, 66
Adolescence: adolescents as crime victims, 13; adult outcomes of adverse conditions during, 67–68, 105; biological risk factors in transitions of, 49–51, 58–59, 133; brains of young adolescents, 51, 133; case vignettes on, 1, 3, 5, 18–19, 46–47, 52, 65, 70, 107–108, 131; environmental risk factors during, 51–60; family relationships during, 51–54; and gangs, 53; and hormones, 50–51; identity crisis during, 48; lack of supervision during, 59–60; Mead on, 48–49; onset of behavior problems during childhood versus, 57–59, 66–67; peer influence during, 52–53, 80, 95, 133; population statistics on, 2; protective factors during, 52; psychologists and psychoanalysts on, 47–51; and puberty, 50; risk factors for delinquency during, 46–69; and school, 54–60; stages of, 49–50; and substance abuse, 2, 56, 58, 60, 62; television viewing during, 23. *See also* Black adolescents; Juvenile delinquency; Latino adolescents
Adoption studies, 31
Adult courts, transfer of juveniles to, 77–81
Adult jails, juveniles in, 70, 78
Adult outcomes for delinquents, 67–68, 105
Advocacy groups, 141
African Americans. *See* Black adolescents
Aggression: adult outcomes of, 67–68; during childhood, 25–29, 108; and exposure to violence, 41–42; gender differences in, 66, 67; and later delinquency, 108; and neurotransmitters, 32–33; and poverty, 39; as predictor of delinquency, 110, 112, 136; prevention program for, 116; and temperament, 30, 32, 35; and testosterone, 50–51
Aichhorn, August, 6, 59, 86

AIDS, 109
Alcohol abuse. *See* Substance abuse
Allen, Joseph, 54
American Psychiatric Association, 4, 61, 64
Anderson, Craig, 42
Angold, Adrian, 131–132
Antisocial behavior. *See* Conduct disorder; Juvenile delinquency
Anxiety disorder: and conduct disorder, 62–63; as internalizing disorder, 63; and poverty, 40; predictors of, 136–137
Aos, Steve, 126–127
Arizona, 14, 70, 76, 124–125
Arkansas, 55
Arrest rate of delinquents, 2, 48, 59, 72, 73
Arrest statistics, 2, 8–10. *See also* Crime; Juvenile delinquency
Attachment, 35–36, 112–113
Attention deficit hyperactivity disorder (ADHD), 1, 6, 18, 34, 60–62, 66
Automobile accidents, 2
Automobile theft, 3

Babies. *See* Infancy
Bandura, Albert, 41–42
Beck, Aaron, 99
Behavior disorders. *See* Conduct disorder
Behaviorism, 86–87, 106
Berra, Yogi, 131
Biological risk factors: in infancy and early childhood, 29–35; in transitions of adolescence, 49–51, 58–59, 133
Bipolar disorder, 83
Black adolescents: bias against, in juvenile justice system, 16; firearms used by, 16; incarceration of, 16; in juvenile detention facilities, 83; population statistics on, 15–16; poverty of, 16, 41; pre-adjudication detention of, 81; statistics on delinquency of, 10, 16. *See also* Juvenile delinquency; Race
Blos, Peter, 49–50